FAITH IN WORDS

TEN WRITERS REFLECT
ON THE
SPIRITUALITY OF THEIR PROFESSION

Christopher D. Ringwald

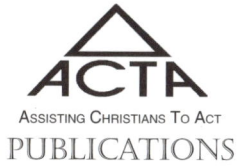

ACTA
ASSISTING CHRISTIANS TO ACT
PUBLICATIONS

Faith in Words
*Ten Writers Reflect on the Spirituality
of Their Profession*
by Christopher D. Ringwald

Christopher D. Ringwald is a graduate of Georgetown University, where he was given the annual journalism award. He earned a master's degree at the Columbia University Graduate School of Journalism and has worked since 1989 at the *Times Union* in Albany, New York. His series on the Iroquois Indians won the top Hearst Newspapers award for 1990, and his reporting on drug and alcohol rehabilitation programs led to a state investigation and new legislation. Ringwald has written poetry for literary journals and articles on social and religious topics for various publications.

Edited by Francine O'Conner and Gregory F. Augustine Pierce

Cover Design by Tom A. Wright

Typesetting by Garrison Publications

Copyright © 1997 by Christopher D. Ringwald

Published by   ACTA Publications
                  Assisting Christians To Act
                  4848 N. Clark Street
                  Chicago, IL 60640
                  800-397-2282

All rights reserved. No part of this publication may be reproduced or transmitted in any form or by any means, electronic or mechanical, including photocopying and recording, or by any information storage and retrieval system, without permission from the publisher.

Library of Congress number: 97-072106

ISBN: 0-87946-161-6

Printed in the United States of America

01 00 99 98 97   5 4 3 2 1   First Printing

Contents

Introduction / 1

One / 11
SUZANNE STREMPEK SHEA

Two / 25
JIM DWYER

Three / 39
PATRICIA HAMPL

Four / 55
PATRICK REARDON

Five / 77
JAN LARSON

Six / 89
DAVID SCOTT

Seven / 97
ALAN ABBEY

Eight / 109
PATRICE GAINES

Nine / 125
ANTOINETTE BOSCO

Ten / 139
TERRY ANDERSON

Faith in Words
is dedicated to my mother,
Margaret Furey Ringwald,

and to the memory of my father,
Eugene Carl Ringwald,

who lived their faith and gave it to me.

Introduction

Writers write to say something they believe no one else is saying or has said. Whether reporter, novelist, editor, poet, publicist or speech writer, each writer secretly believes he or she has a piece of truth to convey. Writers strive, as do we all, toward completion—what the religious call the basic impulse to be one with God. Writers do this on a page, in words, phrases, sentences and paragraphs, each filling in a fraction of the great mosaic of life. "This I know and must tell," the writer shouts.

The present age challenges the writer with an audience more or less indifferent to the printed word. Image and icon, shorthand for thought, reign. At the same time, technology zaps communications—news, novels, home pages, correspondence, research—around the globe. Today's scribes must strain to reach the functionally illiterate while trying to retain the computer-glutted elite.

In the midst of that daily effort, a writer may ask: "Why am I here in front of this typewriter, alone in this mountain cottage or cold-water flat? What does God want of me and what role does faith play in my life and work? Is there a higher purpose to my writing—and did I keep that in mind for just one minute today?"

Many books have been written about writing. Some touch on the faith behind the work; others expound upon religion writers, per se, or novelists and poets who are overtly religious in their work. This book asks a variety of working writers and journalists to describe how they developed their beliefs and allowed their faith to guide their work and life.

Writers of faith can plumb the deepest issues confronting humanity: Why are we here? Do we bear any responsibility for our fellows and the earth? Is there a God and what does God want?

Such questions do matter. Fiction suffers when the writer pretends they never arise. Poetry languishes at some superficial level, no matter how beautifully crafted and written. Not that every work need tackle the profound and sublime, but all writing is improved by an invisible consciousness of the larger issues.

Journalism suffers even more, especially given its long ignorance of religion and spirituality. Seasoned skeptics and neutral observers that we are, we fear believers who believe too seriously. When faith has consequences other than the obvious efforts such as feeding the hungry, we squirm. Those whose beliefs drive them to live in true poverty, chastity or obedience, to blockade abortion clinics or missile plants, to have nine children and home- school them all, to protest condom distribution, to eschew work on the Sabbath, or to isolate themselves from the rest of the world—these we mistrust, mock, and usually ignore. They upset the little cocktail party attended by us reasonable, witty journalists and our ideal readers.

Most writers have a positive horror of being uncool, of having emotions, of being caught off guard. The virtue of fairness has become, in the modern age, that of objectivity. Its ancillary product is a cult of detachment, furthered by the transience and professionalism of the modern workplace.

In this book are profiled ten writers who have broken free from this cult of detachment, who have allowed their faith to inform and define their work.

The struggle is not to write about one's faith so much as it is to live it. Often these writers did not have the luxury of expressing their belief directly. Most wrote on topics other than faith and religion. It seems more compelling to know how Alan Abbey, a devout Jew, former investigative reporter, and now business editor, fulfills the dictates of his conservative Judaism than it would be to hear someone like the Reverend Andrew Greeley expound on his faith, already explicated in a profusion of columns, books and novels. David Scott, who moved from assistant editor of a diocesan paper in Albany, New York, to editor of the well-regarded national weekly, *Our Sunday Visitor,* talks passionately about producing in the religious press the same high standards, compassion and dedication some would expect only in daily secular journalism.

Toni Bosco—author of six books, award-winning editor of a weekly newspaper, and syndicated columnist—was my first interview. Her passion, clarity, and willingness to explore her principles inspired me throughout the project. Jan Larson, a devout Lutheran, decided she had more to offer as a journalism professor than a regular scribe and left the cynicism of the newsroom to spend more time with her family. To her students, she brings the mature values and practical wisdom developed during years of hard-nosed reporting and editing. Patrick Reardon, urban affairs writer for *The Chicago Tribune,* mixes his love of cities with a sound conscience and hard work. His remarks show all three.

Some of the writers are more well-known, such as Terry Anderson, the former Associated Press Mideast Bureau chief who spent seven years as a captive of terrorists, or Patricia Hampl, the poet and memoirist, or Jim Dwyer, the Pulitzer Prize-winning columnist for New York City's *Daily News.* Patrice Gaines, a *Washington Post* reporter, broached the subject of her painful past in a well-known article that helped many troubled young women and then went on to write two books on her experience.

Each of these writers thought long and hard about how to live out their faith through their writing. Suzanne Strempek Shea, a good reporter turned excellent—and successful—novelist, transcended the constrained world of daily journalism to enter the profession that D.H. Lawrence considered the only one capable of grasping the fullness of modern life, of getting it "whole hog"—the writer of fiction. Even in her reporting, now left behind, she was guided by a full set of moral and practical yardsticks.

If nothing else, writers who are religious believers or

seekers appreciate those elements in others. Having explored and embraced their own spiritual identity, they are better able to explore the moral and religious dimensions of their subjects. They are also more able to give such motivations proper perspective, neither demonizing people nor idolizing them. The author and political commentator Juan Williams made the following point about his own work, and the message could stand for every type of reporting and writing.

"Politics is a lot of clanging and noise, an empty sound, without substance," he told me. "What happens on a deeper level, with God and reality, is where the real action takes place. Apart from all the lying and deceit and money changing hands, there has to be a point of reality, of 'Where are you going and what are you doing for your fellow man, and how are you representing God on earth?'"

Consider the audience for these writers: ninety percent of Americans profess belief in some higher power; eighty percent pray regularly; seventy percent identify with a particular tradition; and forty percent attend services in any given week, according to a survey by the Freedom Forum. Other polls show similar results. Glancing at the mix of most daily news, however—crime, politics, weather, sociology, sports—one wonders if editors believe the opposite about the interests of their readers. The same is often true of much contemporary fiction, where characters wander through desolate social landscapes only to reach some affectless apotheosis as the story's climax. "Religion is a determining element in the human story, a powerful ingredient of the social mix," George Cornell, longtime religion writer for the Associated Press, once wrote: "To disregard religion in chronicling any story prevents any intelligent perspective on conditions in this society or any other."

Writers are predisposed to disappointment and frustration. Most are cynical idealists or idealistic cynics, depending on the mix of those qualities. But, from novelist to poet, writers live with the belief that they can make a difference, that their words will tilt or right the world's spin in some small way, even if only for themselves. Alfred Kazin, the great American literary critic, wrote in his memoirs, *Starting Out in the Thirties*, of exploring the world of books with the ideal that "art and truth and hope would yet come together."

Fear dogs every writer's every step. In the introduction to her useful and lovely book, *Walking on Alligators: A Book of Meditations for Writers*, Susan Shaughnessy confides: "Every day I think, 'Today's the day I won't be able to do it.'"

Yet the deepest and simplest aspiration of a reporter, writer, poet or journalist may be to help in some way. The goal is easily ridiculed and helplessly vague; it is also an eternal spring that invariably brings up fresh water. As Sharon Olds said of Whitman, "He made the human race look like a better idea."

A cottage industry has developed around demonstrating that certain creative professions draw people who, while bright, are often psychologically impaired. Dr. Felix Post, a British psychiatrist, studied one hundred writers and concluded they were prone to depression. Though many writers pooh-pooh these speculative endeavors, they do admit that the pressure to create can tax the best constitution. "You wake up every morning and say, what am I doing? What is the point?" Anne Hollander, president of the PEN American Center, said in an interview with *The New York Times*. "I am going to have a drink. I am going to shoot myself."

There is hope. Anne Lamott has an excellent volume for all writers, from the struggling diarist to the published professional. Her book, *Bird By Bird: Some Instructions on Life and Writing*, both instructs and encourages. In it, she says that writing is about telling the truth—a useful reminder to all writers.

The writing life is difficult. We need strong egos, but not big ones. Big egos get in our way; strong ones allow us to go on with courage, conviction and confidence. Many find that faith in God helps. The writers in this book agree, some with certainty, others with only the strong desire of someone stumbling through a dark room knowing that a door waits, somewhere, on the far side. In writing, as in life, something must be at stake. Even fluff should count for something, if only to entertain or stretch. Writing should never be an empty exercise. The pertinent question, as a friend of Anne Lamott asks, is "How alive am I willing to be?"

When much is at stake, an anchor of faith grounds all writers' exploration and experimentation. "This will mean something; this will have some result," we whisper to ourselves. Faith gives perspective and direction. Paul Ingrassia, a Catholic who won a Pulitzer Prize for a series on General Motors management, said in an interview, "There's no substitute in my line of work for sound Judeo-Christian values. They help you keep your role and your job in perspective, and help you recognize the power you have to help or hurt people."

"Your values help you find news and help define what is news and what is not news. You can't write falsehoods, you have to strive for the truth and intellectual honesty," Ingrassia maintained. Good writers, by asking questions, keep uncertainty alive. They embody the rare but radiant quality described by John Keats as "Negative Capability, that is, when man is capable of being in uncertainties, mysteries, doubts, without any irritable reaching after fact and reason...." Good writers cannot always explain or understand everything, in spite of the omniscient presumption of some journalists and novelists.

The poetry of Patricia Hampl hints at the edges of struggles and epiphanies that even she finds hard to explain. As Samuel Hazo, poet and teacher, wrote, "Poetry exists to say that which is as inexplicable as it is undeniable."

Faith can help the writer to see things whole. Daily life militates against such an urge and seems easier if we set people into camps. But it is newsworthy when divisions are not as great as we thought. I once wrote an article examining how altruism, rather than conflict, governs relations between young and old, despite considerable hyperbole to the contrary.

Though it appeared that in local school budget votes older citizens and young parents opposed one another's interests, more in-depth interviews revealed that both groups were eager to accommodate the concerns of the other. A pair of sociologists, John Logan and Glenna Spitze, found the same in surveys they used to write a valuable book, *Family Ties*. But such stories do not make readers clutch their chests and cry out over their morning coffee.

Writers bear the responsibility to think, to break out of convention, to resist editors and publishers and routine. They need discipline to resist the cheap and easy, to avoid being distracted from the deeper truths. Brian Dickinson, who continued writing columns for the *Providence Journal-Bulletin* after being left speechless and virtually paralyzed by Lou Gehrig's disease, once said, "The amazing riches of the imagination lie waiting to be tapped but are often hidden in the daily noise of instant news."

An annoying characteristic of newsrooms and gatherings of writers is a certain weariness borne of being right, being proved right and, nevertheless, being ignored by society as it blunders along.

The cult of knowing this or that tip a day or five minutes before someone else, of having and breaking "news," begins to infect even daily conversations between writers. We are conditioned to a certain type of neurosis, of living in the immediate past and emerging present. Life flies past, and we grab at fragments to somehow represent it all.

The preoccupation with what is "new" compels many journalists to forget yesterday, to toss the past into the recycling bin. Small developments and changes are plucked from the earth and shown to readers—look!—as if they were vegetables planted and grown in one day. Each day, however, follows a few million before. Each news item has a history. It is our responsibility to explain this to our readers. Without doing so, we render the world incoherent and chaotic and drive its residents further into confusion and despair. How can a writer, of fiction as well as of news, resist the fierce temptation of the new, the glittery, the titillating, to which we attend almost always at the expense of the truth?

In the other direction, this urge to know the trivial and temporal can distort our roles as citizens, neighbors, friends and relatives. We journalists are the professional watchers, watching everyone else do.

Robert MacNeil, formerly of the *MacNeil/Lehrer NewsHour*, warned of this danger in a speech: "Democracy and the social contract that makes it work are held tight together by a delicate web of trust, and all of us in journalism hold edges of the web. We are not just amused bystanders, watching the idiots screw it up."

Alas, print made popular democracy possible through its efficient spread of ideas, opinions and news. Print then, in all its modern forms, regularly betrays democracy—or at least seems to—by using its trusted spot to exploit, pander, trivialize and distort the issues of the day. Can a writer be so anchored in faith that she or he can partake of citizenship, rather than merely watch and scoff?

The perspective of faith can help us see the whole. A person of faith is likely to better understand, question and describe the values that motivate our subjects and readers. He or she is likely to know that some point of principle always underlies action and word.

Though many of us presume people act out of self-interest, consider all the decidedly uneconomic decisions people make—such as choosing a suburban lifestyle or giving to charity or being a mentor to a disadvantaged youth. Election campaigns and polls show that people consistently vote on the basis of issues more moral than economic in nature: sexual equality, abortion, gay marriages, civil rights. Even the demands for lower taxes are a symptom of a larger, moral issue: the conviction among many conservative Americans that government has and will do bad things with their tax money. Yet writers brush off or ignore these deeper motivations.

Once, at lunch, several colleagues and I were discussing an important union chief, a leader in the local Democratic machine. They wondered how, despite his political heft, he managed to seem like such a nice, decent guy. I ventured an opinion: "I understand he's a devout Catholic."

They stared at me, as if I had attributed the qualities to his hairdo, and turned away.

"And his brother is the same way, very decent," one man added, as if to clarify the situation but without offering a shred of explanation. Journalists do not have to engage in street-curb psychoanalysis to explain what drives the people of whom we write. Novelists and readers alike know that character is motivation revealed in action. And what motivates some—but not all—people are their religious faith and practices.

Of each writer in this book, I asked a basic round of questions:

Do you believe in God? Why? How did you find your God? What does God want of you? How do you regard the religious beliefs of others, your subjects, and your readers? Do you see these as the basis for their lives? Does your faith provide a practical code of ethics for daily life? Does it provide an agenda for your work? Does it matter that you believe in God? Can others tell that you do? How do you sustain your faith, especially in a lonely, competitive, often low-paying line of work? How do you remain a decent person? How far will you go in fulfilling the vision your faith provides?

As you will see, the conversations veered off in various directions, but each writer shared the how and why of his or her personal belief and where that belief fits into his or her life and work. That is what I was searching for, and that is what I have tried to capture here: their faith in their words.

ONE

Suzanne Strempek Shea

Novelist, former reporter

One reader's reaction to a single sentence she had written made Suzanne Strempek Shea's journey from small-town reporter to successful novelist worthwhile. The line appears at the end of Strempek Shea's first novel, *Selling the Lite of Heaven*, which went into multiple printings and movie rights. In a marvelous epigram, the main character concludes: "I find I can do nothing but believe."

"A woman in Chicago told me that she wrote the last line on a card and carries it with her,"' said Strempek Shea. "If the whole book came together so one person could read that one line, that's worth it to me."

Though success did not come to Strempek Shea overnight, at the age of thirty-five it was certainly unexpected. "I didn't see any of this coming. I wrote about three or four short stories, and this was going to be another. It's a story about a woman's attempt to sell her engagement ring in the want ads after her boyfriend leaves her for the priesthood. This effort provides the coming of age for that woman, who is in her thirties, and she becomes her own person. In the end, she is better off having not married the guy."

Before and while writing the novel, Strempek Shea worked for the *Springfield* (Massachusetts) *Daily News*, which later merged into the *Union News*, writing features and covering several towns. She has since left journalism to concentrate on her next novel, *Hoopi Shoopi Donna*, published in May 1996 and then in paperback.

This second book was conceived in her childhood, when Strempek Shea's father encouraged her to start an all-female polka band. The title comes from the main character Donna's favorite polka, *Hupaj Shupaj Dana*.

"I grew up opposite Pulaski Park, the 'Polka Capital of New England,'" Strempek Shea explains. "I never started the band, the way my father wanted, but when you write fiction you can have people do whatever you want."

Strempek Shea has always been comfortable with her religious beliefs and, in turn, has been guided and inspired by them. She grew up in a Polish Catholic neighborhood in Three Rivers, part of the town of Palmer in central Massachusetts. Strempek Shea, a tall, energetic woman, has a manner both gracious and infectiously optimistic. She and her husband, Tommy Shea, live in nearby Bondsville.

"People are having such a great response (to the first book) because things in the book are ringing true for them," she says. The second book is getting similar reactions. "I basically wrote what I know about. What I put in the characters is what I have in myself: faith that things are going to be all right.

"Without believing there is something after this life, I can't imagine it. The characters in the novel are basically people trying to be nice. The people at the publishers were asking me, 'Do you really know people like that, who are in church every other day?'" She laughs at this collision between the devout, ethnic Catholicism of a New England mill town and the skeptical secularism of big-city editors.

The first novel's protagonist is an endearing young woman whose clear perspective on her Polish parents, Edna and Stanislaus, their uncommunicative marriage, and the workings of church and society in her small mill town is relieved by her love and humility. The novel begins with her fiancé leaving her for the priesthood. The tale then alternates between her adventures of living at home, trying to sell the engagement ring through the classifieds, and flashbacks of the romance. Strempek Shea's greatest gift is to bestow a humanity on each character that prevents any one of them from being unbearably good, bad or tiresome.

The fiancé, stiffly kind and earnest in the manner of a middle-aged bachelor trying to entertain a brood of young nephews and nieces, is saved from being too pure by simple touches. The mother, bothersome and mean-spirited for obscure reasons, has moments of charity or at least devotion. She bows her head when someone mutters blasphemously. Sometimes a third party points out the mother's strong side. The daughter confides to her fiancé, "She didn't give me any goals other than being good."

"Well, that's one fine goal," the young man replies.

The mother's cold and suspicious character is often blunted by her comic aspect. "Wonderful sale. You should have gone," she tells her daughter one Saturday after a parish fundraiser. "We picked out what we thought you'd like, but if it's not the right things, you have only yourself to blame for not coming along."

Late in the novel, Andy, a young man who had given the protagonist a dime-store ring when they were both fourteen, reappears to look at the five thousand dollar diamond ring she is now selling. In an affecting scene, the two discuss the paths of their lives since they last met and the irony of meeting again under these circumstances. Andy has a gift for blurting out maladroit truths. His observation on the two rings she received, one at the age of fourteen and one for a now-broken engagement, transforms the occasion.

"'Maybe,' he said to me, not taking his eyes off the ring, 'in both cases, it was supposed to happen like it happened. At least you saw, twice, that somebody cared a whole lot. Even if one of the times wasn't as big a deal as the other, that's two times more than most people see something like that.'"

The remark sets the main character back and kicks off a liberating epiphany. She is soon able to reject her mother's negativity, albeit under her breath, force a new admirer to admit the nature of his feelings, and move on with her life. The coming of age is all the more powerful given a protagonist so understated that her name is never revealed to the reader. Her main role is that of an observer whose passivity is transformed by an acute, appropriating vision. By naming things and people, we appropriate them. This comes close to being a central theme of both the novel and the writer's life.

One can spot an innately Catholic, incarnational aspect to Strempek Shea's novel. The narrator, and thus the reader, are forced to listen, pay attention, and see life and people as they are. In so doing, we see their divine qualities. Some of that is achieved structurally. By casting the novel as the record of the people coming to look at the engagement ring, we are treated to the stories of prospective customers, who unload their emotional burdens in the manner of Chaucer's pilgrims.

"It is a morbid curiosity, but these people come into my house and I almost have no choice. Here, someone is saying to me: 'Hold this book on embalming and I'll be back in an hour.' Who would not want to take even a quick peek?"

The Canadian novelist Douglas Glover once said that the great thing about writing fiction is that it allows us to be generous and loving in a way we could never be in real life. In *Selling the Lite of Heaven*, whenever people are on the verge of being bothersome they are redeemed by the perspective of love or, more directly, by a love they possess that is, at the same time, beyond them.

These characters have been especially appreciated by Polish Americans, who are more used to seeing their ethnic group memorialized in punch lines to bad jokes. Strempek Shea told one newspaper, "People are coming to me with tears in their eyes saying it's wonderful to see a book that happens to be about Polish Americans and that's funny but is not making fun of them."

Her faith, aside from informing her work, also freed her to embed the lives of her characters in the church and its seasons: "We met in church," the narrator says of her temporary fiancé. "In the vestibule, to be exact."

Later, the man suggests they take off from work on the Feast of the Assumption to have a picnic. The protagonist has a flashback to her fourteen-year-old suitor, who sticks a cheap ring on her finger and then has to rush off: "Gotta go—confession begins in fifteen minutes and I gotta drive the old lady over there."

Strempek Shea's willingness to deploy such touches is coupled with an affective recall of the sacramental life in old-fashioned Catholic communities.

Every Sunday morning, the narrator's parents leave three-quarters of an hour early for Mass so they can get the same pew, fifth from the rear on the left. The saintly fiancé, who later becomes a priest, is the sort of boy who practiced saying Mass in his basement, using his mother's ironing board as an altar. Years later, he chooses the seminary instead of marriage after seeing a statue of the Virgin Mary give him the nod. And his first homily in the home parish is broadcast over the radio, preempting the *Polka Explosion* program.

In her own life, Strempek Shea says that Mass and other devotions, while critical, "are not all my religion is to me. I am grateful for every moment, for my parents and my husband. I am very much a there-but-for-the-grace-of-God person."

Her outlook was shaped early by a death that sharply etched on her consciousness the limits and possibilities of life.

"As far as I know you only get one ride, and it could be over at any moment. When I was in my early twenties, my best friend was killed in a car accident. I realized, 'Yeah, it could be any day for me.'"

Her book, Strempek Shea admits, unabashedly includes

religion as a part of people's lives. "It's not a freak thing. Where I grew up, the Polish, French and Irish immigrants and neighborhoods all had processions, festivals, feast days. It was very Old World. For me, it was nice to share that. Now all these people are reading it and saying, 'When I was a kid, we did that.'"

To Strempek Shea, the big question is: *Why am I who I am?* "I always felt I was the luckiest person in the world, even before this happened with the novel, just in the people I have around me. Most of the people I attended first grade with, I can still see if I drive down the street."

Strempek Shea grew up in an apartment upstairs from her mother's parents, so intergenerational living is entirely familiar to her. In fact, the community depicted in *Selling the Lite of Heaven* is remarkably like the one she grew up in — and where she now lives. In the book, the main character worries about her home town in a manner so touching that the reader cannot but help presume it is shared by the author.

"You still live here?" friends invariably ask the narrator at high school reunions. She thinks to herself: "I am here as I always have been. Sometimes I think that if everybody left after high school, who would live here? Then I think that maybe people who left other towns after high school would have moved here, and when their kids graduate, those kids will leave for somewhere else. Sometimes I think like this and I get a headache."

One can see that the novel is a product of a special life, deliberately lived. Perhaps it was Providence, all along. "God, for some reason, has been looking out for me," Strempeck Shea says. "I always have had a great support system because so many people around me were always praying for me. I almost died from pneumonia when I was a week old. The prayers started then." As a result, Strempek Shea is comfortable with questions of religion and spirituality. "My first memory of God is looking up at the ceiling at a decorative plate, the kind they used to block off the old opening for a stove pipe. I remember my grandmother pointing to the ceiling, telling me about God in heaven. Even when I see one of the cover plates now, I think of her and God."

She recalls help coming in moments of trouble in ways as small as a prayer in a book. "Sometimes I have been in very providential situations." In a troubled, lonely moment, Strempek Shea found a bookmark dedicated to Our Lady of Czestochowa with the reassuring prayer that "Our Lady will always take care of you, just like parents you can go to with anything."

Her urge to put words on paper came at the age of eight: "I got into writing because I found it a lot of fun. My parents went polka dancing every Saturday night, and I stayed with my grandma. I would write out this newspaper, *The Nutty News*, and leave it on the back step for my parents. Even as a kid, I always had stories going on in my head."

Even today, Strempek Shea finds grist for fiction in the minutiae of daily life. One story came from a matchbook ad for tractor-trailer driving school. Her novel began when she noticed a classified ad for a used engagement ring.

"I often look in the classified ads or yellow pages for ideas for feature stories. It's my favorite place." In the novel, the classifieds feed the overheated imagination of the narrator, who finds her ad jazzed up from the copy she submitted.

"I imagine the classified ad clerk, a frustrated former reporter who had begun her career on the obituary desk but who never got past that point because of the one incident in which the newspaper had been sued because, in the interest of sensationalism, she had inserted the word suicide into the obituary of someone who had not taken his own life. Demoted to the classifieds, she vented her creativity there by adding six or seven free words to the beginning of otherwise unimaginative advertisements. Like mine."

Ultimately, says Strempek Shea, writing and journalism are the things "I know how to do the best." She got her start covering high school hockey games for the local newspaper. At the matches, she met her future husband, who was covering sports for the *Springfield Union News*. That contact and her ability to work on weekends and in the summers led to a job on the paper. She stayed for thirteen years, until the success of her novel allowed—and encouraged—her to leave for full-time fiction writing. Earlier in her career, Strempek Shea had spent a couple of years as fashion editor for the *Providence* (Rhode Island) *Journal*. She decided the seventy-five-mile commute was taking too much time out of her life and began working full-time for the Springfield paper.

Strempek Shea was originally interviewed for this article while working as a reporter covering the farming and factory towns of West Brookfield, Warren, and Belchertown in west central Massachusetts. Her enthusiasm for the job was rare, given the reigning discontent of most reporters.

"It's a wonderful job," she says. "A newspaper job is a public service job. We are providing people with information they need, whether it's telling them about an important blood drive or about some creepy guy on their board of selectmen. At least they'll have the information. What they do with it is their part."

Comfortable with her own religious beliefs, it was natural for her to consider the spiritual side of her subjects and readers, to take seriously the beliefs of others. But, she warns, describing another's spirituality requires great care: "It's one of the most private things in a person's life."

Accepting that others have religious convictions driving their lives is good journalism, she believes. It involves trying to glimpse, understand and—when relevant—report on a person's motivations.

"I interviewed a wonderful guy who was a recovering alcoholic. He had restored an old school, which had caught my attention. I went to do a story on the house but I really got into him. He had this blackboard on the front porch where he writes messages for the kids at the new school across the street."

Strempek Shea appreciates such blunt reminders. She has a copy of the Serenity Prayer propped up on her computer: "God grant me the serenity to accept the things I cannot change, the courage to change the things I can, and the wisdom to know the difference."

A reporter needs serenity, courage and wisdom when confronting death, crime, tragedy, trouble—whether it's the loss of a family pet, a multiple-car accident, or a politician's indictment on corruption. "You're not meeting people in best of circumstances," she points out. "Usually they're angry, in shock, really riled up. That's what makes news."

And often a reporter is an unwelcome sight. For a person in tragedy, a reporter armed with a notebook and an eager expression only reminds the person that this personal sorrow will appear in tomorrow's paper. "You can't take it personally," Strempek Shea says. "After all, you do show up on the scene of a tragedy...and sometimes you do get in the way."

As a reporter, she tried to keep things in balance. One of her editors posted a headline on the office wall: "Don't kill yourself over a meathead."

"You may be meeting them on the worst day of their life or after something they never expected," explains Strempek Shea. "There are nice times and bad times. You cover the lottery winners but also the four kids who went joy-riding and killed someone." That is partially why, she says, "I'm more of a features person than a news reporter."

Her good nature emerges even when discussing the competition. Many print reporters may follow a story for days or months, only to see television reporters and camera crews appear at the critical scene, in a courtroom or government office, and grab the public's attention. Strempek Shea expresses none of the frustration of many of her newspaper colleagues.

"We have a leg up on them because we have the whole day to put things together, while they have to rush off to cover another story." Plus, the television reporter will have thirty seconds to a minute to report the same story she will have a thousand words to tell, Strempek Shea says sympathetically. Any obnoxious behavior by competitors at a news scene simply "makes for a good story when you go back to the office. I don't get into any shoving matches."

When working at the paper, her agenda was simple. "I like the ability to put the spotlight on people doing good things but whom you would not normally hear about. A lot of people get overlooked. It might be a guy who runs around as Santa Claus at Christmas time giving out presents to kids, or someone who goes out at night and plants flowers without anyone knowing." She said she misses this aspect of newspaper work.

Sometimes discovering good news is hard work, but a reporter can, over time, make clear to readers what sort of stories they are good at covering. Strempek Shea says that by writing about the good deeds of one person, she also helped readers know that she was a reporter to tip off regarding others who deserve attention.

Strempek Shea found filling space in the paper more than just a job. "It's like having a forum to show people that the world isn't going to hell in a handbasket. There are so many good things and so many good people. If my twelve inches of column can lift someone up or give them an idea, that's what I want to do."

Being known as a good-news reporter has its hazards. Strempek Shea talks of appearing on the scene of a story and being told by one subject, "I'm glad you're here; now I know there will be a good job done with this story." The experience reminded her that a reporter must remain detached from news sources. In this regard, fiction offers her a pleasant change both in topics and in the response of readers.

Of course, a reporter can't always write about good

people and brave deeds, but not every dark deed deserves publicity. "I found out things about people and maybe the public knew these things were going on in their personal lives and maybe they didn't. You have to ask, 'How much of a factor in the story is it?' If it's on their own time and does not affect public affairs or if it's not germane to the story, I'd leave it out."

Like every other writer, Strempek Shea made mistakes that hurt. "One time I was very busy...and I gave a woman a whole different last name. The point of the story was to highlight how this woman visited people who were at home alone or disabled. I wrote her a note to apologize, but I can't say I had the guts to call her."

The lesson: "Just don't do too many things at once, because you'll mess up."

As a reporter for the *Union News*, Strempek Shea shared a bureau office with seven people. The atmosphere was good and she knew enough at the time to appreciate it.

"We were all very supportive of one another. There weren't a whole lot of big egos. I must have some sort of foresight to love what I have when I have it. I can't think of a day when I wasn't excited about going into work. There was always something new."

It is this eagerness to live life, to be present, that Strempek Shea is most anxious to convey to others. "I'm going to be speaking to the local National Honor Society, which I was never in," she says with a guilty laugh, "and that's what I'm going to say, 'just try things.'"

In fact, her experience as a successful novelist has made Strempek Shea sensitive to being on the other side of a notebook or camera. Her publisher sent her on a book tour and she has been interviewed for numerous publications.

"I am really learning about myself. You get asked the same things over and over, so I get down to the truth about myself. I think it would be good for all reporters to go through that. In our own reporting, we would be kinder or nicer or go slower."

Some insights have been less than edifying. "On the road trip, I really got to see important people on a different level. The nicest was Katie Couric, the host of *The Today Show*. I was nervous, and she took both my hands and said 'This is going to be really great. I haven't read your book but I plan to.'"

How does Strempek Shea maintain a spiritual life? Prayer and liturgy and faith, she says. "If it's just Mass, that's not enough, though the Mass forces me to sit and think." Given her inclination to stay busy, she appreciates the discipline Catholic ritual provides. While discussing her career and faith, she busies herself wiping kitchen counters. "I can't sit still. Mass and prayer provide time for me to think about what I'm doing and what I am going to do and what I should be doing."

For Strempek Shea, "Church is part of the rhythm of daily life. It's where everything begins and ends." From there, faith moves outward, in the manner of the ancient dictum that prayer shapes belief and belief, in turn, shapes word and action.

"If you have any faith, it should become a part of your life, like breathing," she insists. On a daily basis, she reads from meditation books and from the Bible, but "not anything formal. I am more active in general discussion groups with women."

Living her faith means loving—openly and in the present. "My father died a couple of years ago. While he was here, I always told him I loved him. He wasn't the most demonstrative man, but I'm glad I did. I'm most like my maternal grandmother, who always had something to say. I feel that if you feel something about someone, you should tell them. I'm always saying more than I should, but so what?"

How about encouraging others, either those of faith or those with little? Strempek Shea says she once tried to boost the spirits of a boss "who was falling into the burned-out category." While still working for the newspaper, Strempek Shea was a veteran in a bureau full of new people and tried to encourage them as well.

But preaching is not her style. "It's better to live by example. I stopped eating meat but I don't mention it unless it comes up, then I'll tell someone why. Or there was one woman who told me about a person she loved who was undergoing surgery. I said, 'I'll say a prayer for you.' She didn't say anything then, but later she sent me a thank-you."

Strempek Shea characterizes herself as "basically happy. My response to having all this goodness in my life is...share it. All these people are writing me, saying this sentence or that in the book will be their motto."

So yes, Strempek Shea says, we are each here for a reason. "Everyone has something. Everyone has a box of crayons. You know, when you're little, you get the box with the rows of crayons and it smells so good. Well, some people just stare at their crayons and never take them out to draw."

Even now, with both novels doing well and readers asking for more, Strempek Shea is keeping her perspective.

"I don't think I have a grand mission. In my own way, I want to encourage people to live a little and not be so discouraged. That's why I love it when people say, 'I laughed,' or 'That really helped me.'"

What informs her work is seeing in daily life and normal people the stuff of creation and the promise of redemption. *Selling the Lite of Heaven* begins with a vision that love coupled with joy can be achieved on earth. On the last page, the narrator has realized this hope. Near the end of the novel, an odd woman who has prodded the main character toward maturity and independence reappears, buys the ring, and sets the narrator free: "'To be awake is to be alive,' she said. She gave my hand a squeeze, then whispered, 'Thoreau.'"

In an interview with the *Amherst Bulletin*, Massachusetts newspaper, Strempek Shea put her spirituality more humbly: "I love people turning out for things."

TWO

Jim Dwyer

Pulitzer Prize winner, New York Daily News *columnist*

Jim Dwyer doesn't spend a lot of time dissecting his moral guidelines or motivations as a columnist for the New York *Daily News*. He's an old-fashioned Catholic who assumes sin is punished, often and quickly—so he strives for the truth in the manner of those honest enough to admit they may find heaven only by fleeing hell.

"I'm not sure what my convictions are, and I don't think anybody is particularly interested in my convictions," says Dwyer. Because he was shaped by the church's emphasis on the power of words and instilled with an Irish pedigree, telling stories—which is what the best journalists do—comes naturally to Dwyer. Efforts to plumb his spiritual motivations perplex him, however.

"People either have those things built in or they don't," he claims. "As long as you have the ability to feel lousy about something you've done, you're in good shape."

Three times a week, Dwyer's column is read by hundreds of thousands of people in New York City, the metropolitan area, and beyond. The *Daily News* circulates about eight hundred thousand copies daily and more than a million on Sundays. That sort of attention guarantees that errors, laziness or prejudice by a writer earn rapid reprisals.

"My readers are pretty sophisticated and smart, and they'll figure things out for themselves and write in," Dwyer says. "Sheer fear and torment of being embarrassed keep me honest."

Dwyer won the 1995 Pulitzer Prize for his commentaries. He credits his series on HIV-positive babies. Previously in New York State, all newborns were tested for HIV antibodies for public health reasons. But the mothers were not notified of the results in order to protect their confidentiality. A positive newborn will not necessarily develop AIDS, but it does mean the mother has HIV. Dwyer learned of the situation while working at a Manhattan hospice for children with AIDS. He saw several children die from illnesses that could have been treated if their condition had been known earlier. In column after column, he advocated universal testing and notification, an idea resisted by the gay community and abortion rights advocates out of concerns over privacy and prejudice. After considerable debate, state law was changed to require testing of newborns and notification of parents or guardians of the results, and a federal law was adopted requiring states to institute a system for identifying HIV-positive babies.

Though it may contradict the popular image of an honest writer suffering for his revelations, Dwyer insists that seeking the truth and working under basic values lead to professional success and keep newspapers solvent.

"Unless you believe that everything is hopeless, you've got to use your brain to figure out what can be done, and you've got to tell people how and what they can do. That's good for business and it's good for your soul. Things that are good for the soul and for society resonate. They're good for you, for the business, and for the readers. Isn't that funny? Makes you wonder why more reporters aren't doing it."

At his previous paper, *New York Newsday*, Dwyer attracted national attention as the first columnist assigned full-time to cover the subways of New York. He broke into the select world of big city columnists, winning awards and being profiled on the front page of the *Wall Street Journal*. This led to his own general-interest column in *Newsday* and, after the

Jim Dwyer

New York City edition of that paper closed, in the *Daily News*. He assures us he has no personal agenda.

"I keep trying to find things that resonate in the most substantial way and to keep a consistently entertaining and provocative column. I can't be too serious—I can't be too anything other than a good read."

A thirty-nine-year-old native and lifelong resident of New York, Jim Dwyer resembles an older man in his expression and aspect. His square, Irish face is not given to surprise or alarm or worry. He has seen much but been shocked by little. Of medium height, Dwyer simply plants his sturdy frame somewhere on the pavement of New York City—in a housing project or slum, at a riot, or under the earth on a subway line.

Dwyer's education testifies to the success of New York's Catholic immigrants in building up a first-rate school system. He attended a special junior high for talented Catholic students, then Jesuit-run Loyola High School in Manhattan and Fordham University in the Bronx. He also received a graduate degree from Columbia University's School of Journalism.

"I was raised in a typical parochial New York situation," he says, "one that embraces two great traditions: first, the mythology and legends of Catholicism with the stories of faith and heroes and heroines; and, second, the certitude that the universe has been lined up with very particular rules and an exacting history that is precisely defined by your third-grade teacher.

"I spent a lot of years not going to church. Now I go a couple of times a month. My spiritual life has stayed the same, but it's not based on the dogma that the world started in year zero and Jesus came along and started the Catholic Church to be run by the pope."

Though his faith has been rocked and challenged, Dwyer's writing consistently displays the characteristics of hard work, reaching for the truth, serving the readers, and telling a good story. Even at Fordham, as editor of the student paper, *The Ram*, Dwyer showed the mix of acuity, deadpan wit, and searing commentary that was later to inform all his work.

Dwyer enlivens his writing with true reporting, a happy antidote to the opinion-based columns of some of his counterparts, who spend more time in offices than out on the streets. He can capture a situation's ambiguity while presenting a thousand-word snapshot of a moral reality. Dwyer leavens his columns with cynicism and the romantic—or Catholic—belief in the possibility of redemption, of grace available to even the worst scoundrel.

The job of street columnist in New York has a long and rich history. Dwyer won the Meyer Berger Award, named for a famous journalist who pioneered a compassionate and hardheaded dedication to the people of New York. He invariably dots his arguments with examples and quotes from ordinary New Yorkers.

Mention the Port Authority of New York and New Jersey, the powerful regional agency ruling over local airports, bus terminals, harbors, and other transit facilities, and Dwyer will remind his readers that the body has yet to fulfill its original goal of seventy years ago: a new railroad freight tunnel under the Hudson River. When Governor Mario Cuomo announced plans for a "people mover" to convey passengers between Manhattan and Kennedy International Airport, Dwyer ridiculed the scheme's impracticality. He zeroed in on a transparent effort to appeal to business-class passengers who, presumably, would loathe sharing subway seats with New York's proletariat. At the same time, Dwyer reminds readers of a half-dozen other mass-transit projects over the years that were announced with great fanfare and never completed.

During an interview, Dwyer entertains one of his two daughters, balancing her on his lap or reassuring her about worrisome comments he is making. (When he mentions Jerusalem's Church of the Holy Sepulchre, he whispers to her: "You know, where Jesus was buried. No, he's not there anymore, remember? He rose again, at Easter.") He and his wife live in the Washington Heights section of Manhattan, once popular with German Jews and Irish Catholics but now also crowded with young professionals, Dominicans, and other Hispanics. Just finding time for an interview was tough for Dwyer, who works five and a half days a week, up to fourteen hours in one day if the topic merits it.

In chatting about his religious beliefs, Dwyer recalls "one of the most profoundly antireligious experiences I've ever had." After writing about the assassination of Meyer Kahane, the militant Zionist leader, he flew to Jerusalem to cover the funeral, which he half-seriously characterized as "one of the biggest in Jerusalem since Christ was killed."

"After Kahane was buried there was a smallish riot," Dwyer continues, "with stabbings and thousands of people stoning Arabs. I did a color piece and had the next day free. So I went to the Old City section of Jerusalem. This was just before the Persian Gulf War. The *Intifada* was in full swing," he notes, referring to the mass resistance of Palestinians to Israeli rule in the West Bank and Gaza. "There was a strike in the Old City and all the shops were shut down. I was with this Palestinian guide, and we went to see the walls of the old Temple, the Dome of the Rock—those sites."

With violence and chaos surrounding him, Dwyer says, "I was hoping to find something. We went into the Church of the Holy Sepulchre, which is occupied by five different sects. The Orthodox have this; the Roman Catholics have that. The Coptic Christians have the tomb. The proprietor, a man in a cowl, said, 'Come in and look where He was laid. You must touch it.' At this point, I was sorry I was there, but I bent down to touch it, stooping on my hands and knees. When you do that, you put your face right into a big bucket with money. Now, I'm not a person who believes a religion or church can't have donations, so I threw a few shekels in.

"But then the proprietor said to me and my guide, referring to the bloodshed and *Intifada* and riots, 'All this trouble is very bad for business.'" Dwyer pauses here, reliving his speechless reaction to this perspective.

"I saw that all these churches were fighting over real estate, the great churches and religions of the world—Catholics and Orthodox and Jews and Muslims—and they had been fighting there for about two thousand years. It drove me to the edge of despair." At this point, Dwyer reaches into the morass of his despair and the interreligious combat and retrieves his main point.

"So, the next question is, is truth obnoxious to Christian values such as charity and compassion? I used to think it was," he admits. "But I don't think so anymore. In the telling and retelling of our great stories, these values are important to understanding. I think they're true, so I accept them."

But it wasn't for any crusade that Dwyer became a journalist. "It satisfied an appetite of mine. I wouldn't attribute it to any set of ideals. Some people have an appetite for lots of money, and I do to some extent, but it was much more possible for me to do newspaper work."

Dwyer keeps in mind "a great manifesto" he heard as a student at Fordham during a talk by veteran New York columnist Murray Kempton, now also at *Newsday*. Dwyer's editor at *The Ram*, the Jesuit priest Ray Schroth—an author, journalism professor, and former *Commonweal* editor—took Dwyer to hear Kempton at the Commodore Hotel.

"Kempton said that the most important thing about newspapers, and maybe their only value, is that they get left behind on subways, and somewhere on the Far Rockaway line it may get picked up by a fourteen-year-old who is the future Grace Paley or John Updike or Saul Bellow."

Aside from learning that a reporter could shape the minds of anonymous and distant readers, Dwyer left Kempton's talk with another message for journalists: "You're never free from the accidental attention of someone who might know.

You really can be embarrassed into telling truths by someone who really knows the deal."

Reporters who want to check their cheap impulses simply need one experience: to be on the other side of a news story. When a reporter is the subject of a story or knows those being written about, sensitivity flourishes as if by magic. Many reporters know in their hearts that any one of their stories could have been, even in some small regard, better or more truthful. Generally, they comfort themselves by thinking it was a matter of little consequence or that an eight-hundred-word article can convey only so much of an event, situation or person. But they see things differently when the tables are turned. Many are jolted to read a relative's obituary mangled in the most pedestrian manner by a major newspaper. More shocking may be stories written by other reporters about events involving the writers themselves or their friends and relatives.

"It's a common experience for newspeople when something they are personally involved in makes the papers," Dwyer says. "They see how situations can be wildly distorted and how an article can bear little relation to events as they really happened. Normally, since most of the world doesn't know about the events you're covering, you can get away with it on a professional level for a long time. But when things are turned around, it's shocking on a personal level."

Dwyer gives an example of coverage of New York City's public school custodians, who once had wide latitude over how they ran buildings and were suddenly subject to fierce scrutiny:

"My father was a public school custodian for many years, and when I'd see the stuff that was written, it used to enrage me. It was so hostile and belligerent and self-righteously wrong."

Dwyer believes that no routine, no matter how tedious or grueling, should lure a reporter into bad writing. Instead, searching out and confronting difficult truths, even when one seems to contradict another, then reconciling them in an article or column can afford a writer rare intellectual and spiritual pleasure.

"Not only is it good for you professionally and personally, it so happens that it is good for your soul to be a good journalist, because you will be confronted by things in apposition to each other. Then you can have the satisfaction of feeling a new dimension. Just as it can be good for you to find out that something you believed in is not true."

While Dwyer doesn't run a lunchtime discussion group on spirituality and workplace ethics in the newsroom, his simple religious beliefs require hard reporting and honest writing.

"What does that have to do with faith? So again you have the question, 'Is the truth obnoxious to spirituality?' and it's not. What is obnoxious is the half-baked use of other people's situations to make your point or fill your day or get the assignment done."

Isn't that difficult to avoid when there's a newspaper to fill up?

"Not at all, particularly since I have a column, which gives me a great deal of freedom in the selection of subjects. I don't have to do things where I gratuitously kick the crap out of someone. For some kinds of work or reporters, maybe that's an accessible and successful route. I don't think you have to be a rat."

Some reporters or writers, weary of repetitive assignments or eager to make money or short on motivation, slip into bad habits. They exaggerate political conflicts, set up straw men they can easily knock down, or expose the most mundane acts as criminal. In the late 1980s, a successful reporter won a prestigious fellowship partly on the basis of having exposed a public official who had made a series of long-distance, personal phone calls to his sister at public expense. Whether or not there had been extenuating circumstances— such as family illness—did not matter to the reporter.

This could be a case of bad judgment. There are worse crimes more worthy of a newspaper's scrutiny in any locale. At the same time, rare would be the reporter who never made a personal call from his or her office.

Dwyer keeps some rules in mind. "I do try to avoid inflicting pain on the subjects of my columns. I try not to demonize them or personalize my criticisms."

Public figures, he admits, make more tempting targets. "I probably have succumbed, though they deserve the same amount of compassion as anyone else. There are some public figures we know too much about, such as Donald Trump. It does test your willingness to be nice to them."

A second guideline Dwyer calls "a variation on the golden rule: Never write a story you wouldn't read." This suggestion, if violated, could cost a writer his or her audience, credibility and job. Being boring is a cardinal sin. Readers can always turn the page. And if they don't get past the first sentence, a reporter's efforts are for naught.

Writers have a built-in sense that can serve them well: their own reaction to their work. A demanding but competent editor at a small paper in upstate New York told his reporters, "If you find a story boring to write, chances are it's going to be boring to read."

Dwyer's third rule is the matter of remembering that the subjects of news coverage and columnists' attention, no matter how dastardly in appearance, may be acting in good faith or out of the best of intentions. This amounts to another rule Dwyer tries to practice.

"I try to keep in mind what Tom Blessin, a Jesuit who taught me at Loyola High School, said about the principles of Saint Ignatius. One was that we should always expect the best of people." A corollary is to walk in a subject's shoes before making a judgment.

A fourth principle elucidated by Dwyer is that a reporter must understand his or her role. "If you have some appreciation for the place you stand between many, many readers and the very few subjects of your story, then you'll connect the two in a way that's enlightened by the truth. From that everything else follows. You won't make people into evil cartoons or caricatures, which translates into the important virtue of charity. And it keeps you away from different forms of dishonesty, from posing and posturing."

Finally, Dwyer believes the media need to be useful to their viewers, listeners and readers. "I want my columns to be something that can be relied upon. A lot of what you get from papers and television is meant to cripple you, to make you prostrate with unquenchable rage or fear. It is not meant to make you a more powerful person, and you end up getting numb to violence and indifferent to corruption and cynical about opportunities. I think to do the opposite in all those cases is my job—and also to be occasionally funny.

Not for Dwyer is the anticapitalist ethic affected by some reporters and social justice advocates. For papers to go on printing, they have to make a profit.

"You have to find a way to make commercial success with the principles you believe in. You've got to realize that newspapers are like big companies everywhere; they're programmed to make money, and if they don't do that they can't do anything else."

Not that any of this gets a daily going-over in the midtown newsroom of the *Daily News*. Though he credits his editors and colleagues with being adults, open to new ideas, and mature enough to discuss touchy topics without prejudice, Dwyer does not hash over workplace spirituality.

"I don't go around telling people what the flimsy underpinnings of my day-to-day life are, though I will talk about certain situations I may be covering with people," he says. As for religious or moral beliefs, Dwyer says these "are not things that are usefully discussed there. They are things of the heart and not of the head."

Like any reporter or writer with religious beliefs, Dwyer has to cope with being surrounded by professional cynics. Here, he finds discretion the better part of moral courage.

"Catholicism is largely a joke in newsrooms, so nobody asks me about it. I just try to not rant and rave when people carry on about the church."

For an idea of how these "things of the heart" play out in Dwyer's work, consider his treatment in November 1993 of a trio of events he linked in a profoundly moral manner—corporate downsizing, a layoff, and an airplane crash:

"The USAir shuttle had recently laid off eighty-seven people from their ground crew and replaced them with a contractor who employed younger workers, nonunion and without benefits. The USAir workers had been basically older and unionized. Now among the eighty-seven laid off were two guys who used to empty toilets, handle baggage, basically do all kinds of valuable but often dirty work. These two were the heroes when there had been a USAir crash at La Guardia—the plane crashed during takeoff in 1992, on an icy day, and fell into Jamaica Bay. The fuel in the water was burning and these two guys literally jumped into ice and fire to save lives. Later on, they were recognized as heroes by the Federal Aviation Authority. But when everyone was laid off, they were let go with all the rest, even though they were a few months short of retirement age. So they don't get the health benefits and other privileges they would have had if they could have retired normally. It was a plain and simple outrage.

"So why was this happening? Because the USAir shuttle used to be the Trump Shuttle, and the banks gave the company all kinds of uncollateralized loans. They got into trouble when Trump had his problems and the company went bankrupt. Now Citicorp basically owns it and USAir manages the shuttle for the bankers. It would be one thing if the line was not profitable, but it is. Supposedly, they weren't losing money. And no effort was made to get the old ground crew to take a pay cut or for the union to make an offer to help save money, if that was what the shuttle wanted to do. Instead, the workers were thrown out like old parts.

"But it's important to understand how they fit into the scheme of corporate downsizing. It would not have been as useful a story without analyzing how the USAir shuttle was running and trying to see the events that led up to the layoff in terms of the Trump shuttle being taken over by the banks.

"I wrote three columns about it. It was an unbelievably intense amount of reporting—I barely had time to go to the bathroom. The first day I started at eight in the morning and turned in at ten at night."

Dwyer took matters a step further, giving readers who might share his reaction some steps to take on behalf of the dismissed workers. "I also published the names of important people to write to, at the banks and the shuttle. Later, I think Senator Ted Kennedy was trying to do something for them." Dwyer heard from dozens of readers who pulled their savings out of Citicorp or threatened to.

Though the situation seemed black-and-white, there were difficult choices. Dwyer realized it would not be enough to talk with the two laid-off heroes, that he should check with others. "There was a woman they saved who was badly injured in the crash. Now they didn't want me to contact her, since they wanted her not to be disturbed and they were afraid an interview would bring it all back. But I called her anyway. After all, she could have hung up if she didn't want to talk with me."

Though eager to do good, fear of punishment also motivated Dwyer in his work on the layoffs. "It could have been that USAir was really trying to preserve jobs. I could have been a sucker. It would have been embarrassing afterward to find out they were doing something painful but good for the company and its workers. But, as it turns out, that's not what happened."

Almost alone among New York columnists, Dwyer champions the basis of the city's prosperity, law and order, neighborhoods and life: jobs. In column after column, he gives readers the grim facts on the city's loss of factory jobs. The legions of working-class people who populate the outer boroughs and form New York's foundation are not finding salvation in the computer age. Even the more general service economy is crashing.

"In the postindustrial age, especially in the northeast, service-type jobs were in abundance for years," he points out. "We became, during the 1980s, very skillful at creating that sort of work. But now they're automating those sectors and making labor superfluous. So what was seen as an alternative to the industrial economy is turning out to be a bust."

Calling this trend one of the most profound and damaging shifts in the economy, Dwyer says more reporters and commentators should be covering it. Better to talk about jobs than simply pound the law-and-order drum.

"I don't believe in more jails and more cops; that's a waste when people aren't educated or working. The new mayor thinks police commissioner is the most important job, and there's all this *Sturm und Drang.* That's a waste. The most important job he can create is for someone who will figure out how to make more jobs in New York, and that will do more to cut crime than all the nine-millimeter guns you can buy for the police."

Though a secret set of ideals may shine inside his soul, Dwyer credits his hard work to "an enormous ability to feel rotten. Fortunately, with a column I have a quick opportunity to redeem myself."

Despite his protestations, Dwyer clearly has thought out his beliefs and how to practice them. But could a reader, unacquainted with him personally, know this?

"I have no illusions that people follow my *oeuvre*," he says. "What matters more is that they are not getting their intelligence insulted."

THREE

Patricia Hampl

*Poet, memoirist, professor,
1990 MacArthur Foundation Fellow*

"But maybe it's the wrong question," the poet says. That was in response to my *first* question, "Do you believe in God?"

Oh, well. Patricia Hampl—poet, professor, memoirist, 1990 MacArthur Foundation fellowship winner—has, after all, agreed to be interviewed on matters most personal and spiritual.

Hampl lives in St. Paul, near the neighborhood where she grew up and "in the shadow of the cathedral." She teaches at the University of Minnesota. A memoir of her Czech-American background, *A Romantic Education*, remains widely popular. A more recent memoir of her Catholic background and her spiritual quest, *Virgin Time*, was cited by *The New York Times Book Review* as one of the notable books of 1992. Hampl authored two books of poetry, *Woman Before An Aquarium* and *Resort And Other Poems*. In 1995, she edited *Burning Bright*, an anthology of sacred poetry from Judaism, Christianity and Islam.

As a young adult, Hampl also inhabited the work-a-day world of newspapers, even in college. After graduation, she was a copy editor for the *St. Paul Pioneer Press*, then editor for Minnesota Public Radio. She still writes an occasional travel piece and book review.

"I loved working in journalism. It's very satisfying. You

write it, and pretty soon it's there, in the world."

Hampl was born in 1946. Her Catholic childhood was largely one of the solid and secure Church that ended with the Second Vatican Council. This magisterial institution, with its far-flung colonies centered on parishes, monasteries, convents, schools and colleges, provides many of the images of Hampl's writing. In *Virgin Time*, she recalls, "Mine was a Catholic childhood spent gorging on metaphor—Mystical Body, transubstantiation, dark night of the soul, the little martyrdom of everyday life. Maybe we had too much meaning too early."

Yet, as in *Virgin Time* and in conversation, her spirituality, centered on what she calls "an instinct for worship," represents a thoroughly modern but well-grounded synthesis of Western and Eastern faith traditions.

And actually, her first answer to the question of belief in God is laughter, followed by, "Well, for shorthand, yes."

She continues. "I don't think the issue is whether one believes in God, because then one gets into the whole question of proving God's existence or doing an acrobatic act which most people think is faith, where you leap behind the rational into this mist where nobody can reach. This drives the twentieth-century mind crazy because we are so committed to the rational.

"So for me faith isn't about this thing out there. There is, however, evidence that we have an instinct for worship. We know that we have that instinct. We don't need to go beyond our own experience to verify it."

To hear her speak, the "instinct to worship" seems more real, more capable of proof, than God's existence.

Yet the Incarnation, or an incarnational ethic, looms large in her work. Purposely or not, she corrects some of the transcendental excesses of Christianity by emphasizing a God, or at least a sacredness, that is present in daily life. Details noticed are transformed by metaphor. The light in her convent school was not just light, for "nothing was just anything there. The whole place was an injunction to metaphor, to the endless noticing of detail that is rendered into transformation."

Even before Vatican II, Hampl sensed that this fixed and secure world was being shredded in history's turbulence: "We were falling, falling—away from the forms that sustained life."

"A sense of reverence is instinctual, and it exists in people in different ways," Hampl says, then eagerly emphasizes that this does not exclude the atheist or agnostic.

Indeed, these people can possess, or at least manifest, the instinct to an even greater degree. But her own instinct for worship, she notes, was planted and fertilized and pruned in an ancient religious culture.

"Sometimes people who are the most 'irreligious' are actually very reverent. I don't want to deny the fact that I was brought up Catholic. My earliest formation was through a very highly evolved religious institutional church, which I, of course, rebelled against later on. I really was formed through the Catholic educational model, pretty much pre-Vatican II, old-style Catholicism with all the good and bad that that suggests."

Then the question is, how can a writer respect other people's religious inclinations or, in Hampl's phrase, their instinct for worship? How does Patricia Hampl, returned Catholic and product of a rich Catholic childhood, accept others' approaches to the Divine, or at least, to worship? Several qualifiers first, please.

"I think that, even during that twenty-year period when I had no connection with the institutional church and was even adamantly opposed to any involvement with the Catholic Church, a lot of the references in my work had to do with a spiritual understanding of existence," Hampl says.

What transpires at this level, as sages and poets and average believers have known throughout history, is often inexpressible.

"Most writers, particularly poets, are trying to touch the point beyond which anything can be expressed," she continues. "The relationship between silence and language is the great balancing point of poetry, saying the ineffable. When people are seeking God, that's what they are doing.

"That's why you find in contemplative life a great interest in poetry. The minute you begin talking the languages of contemplative life and poetry, the two are easily translated. Like Czech and Slovak, they're close enough to understand each other."

What about Hampl's passage from rebellion to practice? Was it a dramatic return or simply an awakening to her original faith, now refound under a familiar blanket? She describes how she came to realize that her instinct for worship informed her writing and life even during her time away. The struggle is captured in part by some of the poems in her collection, *Resort And Other Poems*.

"I went through a really rough time and during that period I had a searing experience. A lot of attitudes I had just fell away, and I became open and began praying again. When I look back, I see that a lot of my poetry has to do with prayer, but I didn't know that when I was writing the work."

She cheerfully describes herself as a practicing Catholic. Though the phrase may sound exclusive to some and redundant to others, Hampl's explanation makes sense.

"I like the phrase 'practicing Catholic' because faith is a practice rather than something hard to swallow. I don't think faith is about getting over your rational mind."

Hampl gives our relation to the Divine a decidedly human slant. She reorients, dramatically but practically, the relationship, saying, "Faith is based in the human; it does not belong to God but to us."

This is a point embedded early in Hampl's consciousness, according to her memoir, *Virgin Time*. As a girl, one day she helped a neighbor root out some dandelions. In response to her questions, the neighbor admitted he did not attend church. Then, when asked about God, he declared, "God isn't the problem." For Hampl, this opened some "ancient fissure." She recognized that there was a problem and that it was life, not God. She records her feeling of alarm at recognizing the truth of the man's remark:

"This perverse insubstantiality of the material world was the problem. Reality refused to be real enough. Nothing could keep you steadfastly happy."

Faith, like everything in creation, Hampl says, partakes in evolution. "So faith has evolved, and in the twentieth century faith has to look different from the faith that we recognize from previous eras. To my mind, it is natural that in the twentieth century, and soon in the twenty-first, faith includes the experience of doubt."

Faith, she says, occurs in the face of that uncertainty, "and undertakes the pursuit and the search for God anyway. That seems to be the truth about faith in our times."

In the title piece of *Resort And Other Poems*, Hampl introduces this idea of a belief for the modern age:

Forgive me this faith is based on no miracles.

Seeing is believing.

I hope to see. Just that. The rose.

Hampl points out that people raised outside of any faith or religion have their own struggles to resolve these questions. She claims no expertise there. But a faith for the modern age represents a dramatic change for her.

"For someone like me, brought up in a highly defined faith, the Roman Catholic culture of the old style, it feels a little strange that the certainty will never be there again. It just isn't there."

At this, she pauses for a moment, then resumes more slowly. "I've talked to nuns who say, 'We're not sure there is life after death.' These are people who are not supposed to talk that way. These are totally committed, intelligent nuns who recognize that this is the way things are for us today."

Listening to Hampl, I realize that the struggle for faith may have more substance, paradoxically, in an age of doubt. People today are less likely to believe just because mother or father or pastor, rabbi, or imam told them to. With increased appeal, freedom and skepticism beckon to each potential believer, something I have both experienced and have seen in many friends. Hampl found evidence of a greater substance in modern quests while compiling works for *Burning Bright: An Anthology of Sacred Poetry*.

"What was interesting about gathering poems from Judaism, Christianity and Islam, was to discover so many sacred poems in contemporary poetry—and that they were much more satisfying and real than poems that had come from ages of faith or pietism."

For her more complete thoughts on the topic, she directs one to the introduction to that book. Here she writes that a "true passion drew the Western mind away from polytheism" and lay under the "urge toward monotheism" of the three major Western religions: Judaism, Christianity and Islam. To this "poignant craving for relation with the One and Only" she directs her, and our, attention and notes that the modern age is marked by a "persistent confession of disbelief."

Here Hampl may describe the new era, one that strikes me as a time of believers comfortable with uncertainty. Many of us have encountered this in the young, which is disconcerting and hopeful at the same time. But some are not so at ease with worshipping a deity about whom they feel unsure. Hence, the sheer wave of doubt, exclaimed publicly and privately, in word and text, by neighbors, politicians and teachers. We are not certain, we wish we were, and in our discomfort we speak at length on that loss rather than about the gain of an uncertainty which may ultimately be more revealing and, ironically, comforting.

In her work and conversation, Hampl captures this tidal change. "The loss of faith, the nostalgia for or fury against religion, are all part of the sacred," Hampl writes in the introduction to *Burning Bright*.

The modern feeling for worship contrasts with the old, when belief was often compelled or a matter of habit. "I make a real clear distinction between faith and piety," she says. "Piety has been burned out of us."

But is this necessarily good?

Yes, to Hampl, who says piety "feels phony to us."

"Piety suggests a model of faith that has at its core unquestioning assumptions and cultural underpinnings that make it easier to see life in religious terms," she explains. "What I found so exciting in the contemporary poems was that nobody was sure of much besides a desire for a connection with God. The search felt ancient, very deep and elemental, and it also felt very contemporary."

One wonders then about the relationship with God. How can a writer know what God is asking of him or her? I ask, how can Patricia Hampl know?

"It's the same for all of us, to find a way to listen. In the Western tradition, the best way is through contemplative prayer and prayers from the Divine Office," she says, referring to the ancient prayers, psalms and other biblical passages known as the Liturgy of the Hours, which structures the life of monasteries, abbeys and convents. Traditionally, it provided for seven times of prayer daily, but today greater flexibility is encouraged. Its revision, undertaken from 1965 to 1975, was designed to make it accessible to all believers.

"That pattern is extremely valuable to us. It clears and focuses the mind."

Faith in Words

In *Virgin Time*, Hampl writes of life in a friend's monastery and the role of the Office in organizing time and placing each day in a long line of days: "This daily round, year after year, decade upon decade, means they are never further than a couple of hours away from the greatest poetry of our tradition. . . . This communal prayer voiced a harmony otherwise elusive in all of creation, yet thrumming in the monastic silence."

Hampl reads the Office, goes on a spiritual retreat annually, and follows the seasons of the church year, participating in the special liturgies and practices of Advent and Lent. While not sure what her spiritual habits have to do with her writing, joining in a church of believers makes a difference in her life.

"I think there is also something about being connected to a people. Despite the strong differences I have with my own church, that is where I have chosen to make my practice. I am sure I could find a less offensive religion."

That last could be a credo for many a devout if reluctant Catholic. As have other prodigal offspring, Hampl talks of returning to and accepting the house in which she was raised, despite its imperfections.

"I believe in acquiescing to your heritage. If I were brought up Jewish, I'd be Jewish, I suppose. Or Muslim if I came from a Muslim family."

Yet her Catholicism is one of many beliefs in the world. She welcomes the diversity, the many paths. "I'm glad that other religions are having an effect in the Western world. Christianity is not the ruling belief system it once was; it does not have the hegemony it once had, and I think that's good. It's good for Christians. We are a 'way' now and we follow our 'way,' rather than claiming our religion as the one-and-only truth."

The phrase echoes what the earliest Christians called their faith, the Way. Told this, Hampl says she likes the ancient church and the modern version's connection to it, but the conviction of the early church that Jesus or Christianity is *the* Way is not for Hampl.

When asked how a writer can take seriously the beliefs of others, she recalls being asked to edit an anthology of Christian poetry. She declined, thinking it too narrow in the world we now inhabit. Offhandedly, she suggested the publisher consider putting together a collection of poetry combining the major monotheistic traditions of the West: Judaism, Christianity and Islam. Later they called back and asked her to do this project instead, and *Burning Bright* was the result.

"I really feel a relationship with those religions and also a deep connection with the meditation practices of Buddhism. I'm not alone in that." Hampl recalls seeing Buddhist prayer mats and pillows, Asian meditation bells, and other Eastern accoutrements in many Catholic monasteries. As did Thomas Merton, the Trappist monk and writer, she welcomes the use of Eastern religious habits by Christians as one of many fruitful cross-pollinations.

This then is the long overdue stage of "religious maturity" of which Merton wrote, one in which a faithful Christian can learn from Buddhism, Hinduism and other—especially for Merton—Asian traditions. Merton thought the combination of the "natural techniques" and graces manifested in Asia with the "Christian liberty of the gospel" would deliver us all to "full and transcendent liberty" beyond cultural and other differences.

"I feel a real connection at the level of practice, and that's where faith exists; it's not a series of opinions," says Hampl. "I feel at that level a buoyancy in my own faith to know that others are free in theirs."

This sensibility, grounded in faith and practice, gives Hampl a remarkable sympathy for the faith search of others. In *Virgin Time*, despite a clear eye on the assorted agnostics, English eccentrics, overwrought devotees, and the sheer mass of eager and desperate faithful she encounters on pilgrimages to Lourdes, Assisi and a California monastery, Hampl depicts each person or type in their humanity and their love of something beyond themselves—God, the rejection of God, the instinct for worship.

"The English tourists in the first part of the book, to a person, were not consciously believers. None of them was Catholic and all were fairly repelled by the excesses of Roman Catholicism. Some people thought I was a little tough on those people. I didn't feel that; I was amused by them. As for the nuns and the priests on the second trip, my whole attempt was to render their faith."

How is this done? By that ancient writer's habit: observation. "If you pay attention to people and notice what they do, that is respect. Attention is respect." Throughout her writings, thumbnail descriptions of uncanny brevity and effectiveness bespeak an almost spiritual level of attentiveness. Of an Italian customs official she writes, "His glance stapled me like a memo crossing his desk, and passed on...." Or of fellow airplane passengers, "...all these strangers reading *USA Today*, entranced as children deep in comic books."

One must push the ego off to the side for the senses to be so open and attuned, something I find hard to do consistently. When successful, even to the slightest extent, I have learned that seeing people act out their faiths is a endlessly rewarding activity. Hampl brings to the observation a keen sense of people's creativity.

"Faith is really an art form," she says.

How so?

"It's a human creation, not something God created. It's our way of trying to express the inexpressible longing we feel for something greater than ourselves. That's why there are so many religions. If you kill one, you stomp out a whole people and a whole history. And that's why people are willing to die for their religions and why other people are willing to kill for them."

Patricia Hampl

Yet others, those who do not confess a belief in God, have their own search, their own faith and instinct for worship.

"I have a good friend who's a scientist, and he thinks I'm nuts. He happens to admire my writing, and he sat me down after *Virgin Time* and said, 'You're such a good writer, why do you write about this stupid stuff?'

"It made me realize that there are some people religion doesn't reach. His idea of belief has to do with this notion of certainty and the rational. Alternatively, and what I find equally repellent, is the idea that belief involves turning off a piece of your mind. I don't think it's about your mind; I think it's about your whole being.

"There's no question, when some people find out I'm a practicing Catholic, my IQ goes down in their eyes about twenty-five points. It's seen as an eccentricity."

Virgin Time ends with a kind of epiphany, when Hampl, praying on a hilltop with other retreatants at a monastery, embraces who she is and what she believes. Even more, she embraces the innocence she finds at her core but has long resisted, even denied. This is somehow entwined with her birth into and her life in the Catholic Church. The moment is one of silence, the virgin time of her title.

Yet one can see, in earlier poetry, this search for the perfect moment of silence and the Divine therein contained. In the poem "Direction" she wrote:

Some ragged gesture,

the wound of too much explaining.

What you need is to stand still,

no mirror, no flower, no future.

Hampl shies away from questions about any personal, ethical code that may be borne of her faith. "I don't know. You hope you live in a way that's decent." She mentions an atheist friend, who has a highly developed moral sense, then continues, "The whole question of morality and faith is a vexed one. You can't count on people of faith to be shining examples of moral courage.

"I find myself reticent to make any kind of claims. I still feel very much like someone trying to practice my faith. This is something I can't put words around. I have no idea what I would be capable of in a pinch. I have certain beliefs and things that I act on that have to do with my faith, but it would be too hard to describe them."

So why write?

"That's an instinct for me as basic as praying. I have always done it; I have always found it a worthwhile and inevitable act. I have never questioned it.

"I met a Catholic priest once who had an unbroken experience with his faith. He was fifty years old, a monk. He was one hip guy, who lived well and beautifully. He had never questioned his faith, never broken with it as I did. He had grown rather than mended. I belong to the broken and mended school. He never questioned religion; he matured in it. That's how it's been for me with writing. My relationship with literature has never been broken since I was a child."

In *Virgin Time*, Hampl says she writes from life and imagination; she writes about the past in order to make it *be* the past. Yet the book also describes the beginning of the pilgrimage that continues into the present and future and is apparently at the center of her life: "I knew that I must set out on the trail. That, too, was instinct...."

Indeed, one reviewer called the memoir, "A journey into silence and prayer, a journey to the past, to the self...." The power of silence is greatly underestimated in our world, but its practitioners and observers know its immense creativity. In a remarkably sympathetic profile of Our Lady of Mount Carmel Monastery in Brooklyn, a Carmelite cloister, *New York Times* reporter Randy Kennedy contrasted the more active social justice work of many modern nuns with the life of prayer and silence of this community. The article concludes with the 1942 observation of a nearby parish priest regarding the monastery: "That which saves society is not that which can be seen upon the surface of things. It is not the power of industry or war, of genius, of letters or arts. It is what touches its depths in a silence called the silence of good things."

Like the spirit, the throbbing force at the heart of reality, Hampl's art goes where it will. There is no agenda, formal or informal, for the work of attending, listening, hearing, recording and expressing.

"I have projects that I'm thinking about doing; some I will do and some I won't.

"Opportunities arise. And there are, as well, ideas that you carry around for a long time. It's sort of like war. There are underlying and immediate causes of war; there are underlying and immediate causes of writing, too. I knew, for example, while writing *A Romantic Education* that I would write *Virgin Time*. I knew when writing about my ethnic past that at some point I would write a book about my Catholic past. They were like a matched set, salt and pepper. I have one other memoir I'm writing, but that will take some time.

"Now I am working on a book of essays about memory, and some fiction. The classic pattern has been to write fiction and then write a memoir. I did it the other way around."

The book about memory stemmed from some early writings on the topic and a growing fascination with the elusive, complex faculty. "It grew out of my own writing but now it's about other people's writing."

Aside from being the natural resource for so much literature, memory itself has fascinated many writers, including this one. To judge from fiction, poetry and my own life, memory can be more important than experience. Culture and identity begin at the point where events become memories and are told and retold in stories whose shape and details change over time but whose substance expresses some primal truth about a person, a family, a nation or humanity. Claude Levi-Strauss, French anthropologist and writer, once wrote something along these lines: "Memory is life itself, but of a different quality."

On more practical matters, Hampl has few guidelines other than discipline and focus. The loneliness of the writer's life has not burdened her. She laughs softly at the notion. "Sometimes it's not lonely enough. As a friend of mine says, 'I don't need any help; I just need to be let alone to do it.'

"I have a husband, nice friends, interesting colleagues and students. My main job is to get myself away from those nice distracting people in order to do some work."

She attends weekly Mass at a contemplative monastery outside Minneapolis. "There are other lay people who do that," Hampl says. "We almost constitute a parish; well, we are a parish."

She remains available to those who seek her out, just as she sits patiently through my questions about matters of faith and work and practice, questions that many successful writers cheerfully avoid in interviews. Hampl teaches courses in memoir and autobiography at the University of Minnesota.

Hampl holds back from encouraging anyone toward God. "My work has to do that," she says. "I felt pretty nervy to be publishing a book about my experience as a Catholic and as a seeker. I didn't feel it would be anything that people would be interested in. I think that's how you help people, by jumping off the high dive yourself and taking the plunge. I'm not much of a proselytizer. My least favorite part of Catholicism is the apostolic part, because I think Christianity has been so wedded to governmental and institutional models, particularly Catholicism. It's done a great deal of evil. I'm a little allergic to that aspect of the church. The wisest and most discerning missionary types these days understand that the mission is not to go out and convert, but in a sense to deepen one's own conversion."

Patricia Hampl

This suggests to me the danger of excessive individualism. Many avenues of spiritual seeking today encourage private search. The literary—and sometime religious—critic Harold Bloom argued that most American versions of religion, from Catholicism to Southern Baptist to the Mormons, are essentially gnostic. Indeed, one of the most common refrains I hear from people who live outside an organized religion is that they believe and pray, "in my own way."

So I ask Hampl, would not this concentration on deepening one's own conversion rather than evangelizing foster a private or individualistic spirituality?

"No, because if you're following a practice, you're connected to a whole people," she explains. "I always think secretly that I'm connected to the globe because there are persons of different faiths all over the globe, praying. That's what I'm connected to.

"In the front of my Bible, I have two pictures, both Muslims at prayer, one in Bosnia and another during the Gulf War in Iraq, bent down with gas masks while praying on Oriental carpets. I don't think, if you give yourself over to a practice, you ever feel, in a bad way, lost in space."

FOUR

Patrick Reardon

Author, Chicago Tribune *urban affairs writer*

Americans, historically ambivalent about cities as repositories of the poor, continue to decamp for the suburbs. Those who advocate for cities are seen as softhearted do-gooders. Patrick Reardon, urban affairs writer for the *Chicago Tribune*, knows he's in for a double whammy, being both a devout Catholic and a fan of the city and its people.

"I'm saved from being seen as too flaky because I am real good at statistics. I'm known as the numbers guy, and also as the city guy who knows it inside and out, the guy who loves the city. Other people love it, but not as much as I do."

The remark is typical of Reardon, a self-effacing forty-seven year old who combines equal portions of head and heart in his personal reflections and work. His love of the city and his good intentions are readily balanced by facts, statistics and hard work; and he is not observing city life from afar. Reardon lives with his wife, Catherine Shiel-Reardon, and their son David and daughter Sarah on the north side of Chicago in Edgewater, just south of Loyola University and adjacent to Rogers Park and Uptown.

"The three neighborhoods together are the most integrated in Chicago, with four ethnic groups: white, Hispanic, black, and Asian." Typically, he knows that in seventeen of the thirty census tracts comprising the combined area, no one group is a majority.

Reardon is a product of Chicago, where he grew up in a large family and a neighborhood where "being Catholic was as expected as being Irish." He attended St. Jude's, a seminary high school run by the Claretian Fathers, priests who are heavily involved in writing and the media.

"I took the high school test for them because it was given earlier than the diocesan high school seminary exam. A nun suggested I do so as an exercise, but I got a scholarship and they had a seminary that was away from home. Since I was from a family of thirteen other brothers and sisters, home was crowded, so the idea of going away was attractive."

He also liked the idea of one day belonging to an order that published such magazines as *U.S. Catholic*. "I saw myself as a priest who would be a writer."

He continued with the Claretians, living in their campus community while attending St. Louis University, a Jesuit college. He then spent six months in the Claretians' novitiate before deciding his vocation lay elsewhere. He got a job at the paper in his old neighborhood. From this soil his own beliefs evolved without drama, "blossoming and being enriched," he says.

"Rather than a discovery, as the fundamentalists talk about, it was more of a continuum. What I believe is not something separate—it's who I am."

What do his beliefs entail?

"At the core, it means treating people well and respecting them. It means you're called to love people and to be trustworthy and honest. Which gets to writing, where you are dealing with truth. As a journalist, you're a truth teller and a truth seller."

As a child, he found he could write. "It was easy," said Reardon. "I just did it, and I got recognized for it real early."

When a neighborhood newspaper held a contest for father of the year, a grammar school teacher submitted an essay he had written. It was published along with photos of Reardon and his father.

The Irish tradition of storytelling and literature is well known. But Christianity and Catholicism are rich in narrative as well. Jesus taught in parables, and much religious faith and doctrine is conveyed from one generation to the next through stories—biblical, personal, lives of the saints.

"I recognize that I'm from the same gene pool as James Joyce and others, but my family is not very poetic or into writing. Neither was our neighborhood, which was very working class. The people who were doing well were politicians. Most working people were cops or city workers."

Reardon's mother was a homemaker and his father was a Chicago police officer. His youngest sister also joined the police. Aside from considering the clergy, "I came within a whisker of being a cop myself," says Reardon. Actually, many an Irish-Catholic city youth has considered the same pair of alternatives. Their similarity is captured in a phrase from a Lawrence Ferlinghetti poem that refers to "cops and other confessors."

After stints at a neighborhood paper and the City News Bureau, a Chicago wire service that has trained generations of journalists, Reardon joined the *Chicago Tribune* in 1976, a newspaper with a daily circulation of six hundred fifty thousand and more than a million on Sunday. For most of that time he has covered the city, its people, and its institutions, a job he fits into easily. "I'm the urban affairs reporter because I love this stuff."

The question is, how does Reardon combine his vocation as a writer with his Catholic faith? More simply, how can a person be a good reporter and a person who lives out of deep moral and philosophical convictions?

"At work I feel like an undercover agent," Reardon says simply. Perhaps it's another manifestation of his twin urges to be Ferlinghetti's cop and confessor, since spying is one motivation to write—to enforce and seek out the truth in often indirect ways. But in Reardon's case, the sense of being undercover stems from his desire to live in faith without waving a cross about the office. Life in a highly secular world is one challenge, but being Catholic and a good reporter in a profession where strongly held values can seem suspect is the greater battle.

For Reardon, more significant than the *Tribune*'s political bent (once a "rabidly Republican newspaper but now more middle of the road") is the professionally "value-free" and detached ethos of journalism.

"There is a certain amount of distance the news media keeps from real life, a certain coolness about what's going on, a certain detachment," he contends.

At the same time, a different ingredient has changed big-city newsrooms. In the 1970s and 1980s, salaries rose such that reporters were no longer drawn from nor fully identified with the working classes. Reporters themselves were more likely to have college and even graduate degrees. The income and class gaps between print journalists and their readers are especially striking because newspapers were once seen as the common person's companion and advocate.

Many *Tribune* editors and reporters, says Reardon, "have a suburban mind-set. They're looking for the good life and not dealing with the realities of the poor or the cities. The *Tribune*, from a corporate and journalistic standpoint, is strong in the suburbs."

The *Tribune* puts out local editions in different zones. As at most papers with zoned editions, the front section, with major local, national and international news, remains the same, as do the sports and features sections. Readers receive more news from their neighborhood, less from other neighborhoods. Advocates of zoned editions like giving people more local news without spending a fortune on newsprint. Critics warn that the tailored versions of a metro paper lead to people in a middle-class suburb reading about their area and poor people in housing developments reading about their area, but neither learning much about the other. Reardon has doubts about zoned editions.

"I see the logic and the need for it. Maybe if you are living in a middle-class suburb, it seems as if it doesn't matter what happens in the city, which might as well be a foreign country."

The geographical divide has consequences. Reardon gives an example of how he tries to ameliorate some of the myopia:

"The editors almost all live in the suburbs. Their idea of grappling with the African-American community is covering the public housing of the Chicago Housing Authority. Now, that's only about eight percent of the more than a million blacks who live in Chicago.

"They also tend to go overboard covering the horror and misery of living in Chicago Housing Authority developments. That shows up in the headlines. It's woven into the culture of the paper. What I try to do in my stories is pump in nuances that go beyond the clichés that go into headlines."

Reardon once succeeded in having a headline changed, which is hard for reporters, who often file their stories and leave before copy editors compose headlines. The headline spoke of "Despair" in public housing. He persuaded editors to change it to something like "Public Housing Residents Have Hard Time Finding Hope."

"Editors have a tendency to roll out words like despair and misery and horror in these stories," Reardon points out. "What gets overlooked is that people do make their homes in Chicago Housing Authority buildings. You see this especially with new reporters who come back from covering a family who lives in a CHA building and write a story about how meticulous their housekeeping was, as if being poor means they are going to be sloppy."

This is one reason Reardon prefers to put his home where his heart is, in a racially and economically integrated city neighborhood.

"The race fears that get raised in all-white neighborhoods don't get raised here. One beauty of where we live is that my kids' main baby-sitter for years has been a Filipino grandmother. They have friends who are black and Serbian and Hispanic."

Today, Reardon's religious faith informs his life and work in several ways. "At work, it is hard to be a believer among cynics. I'm there looking at things in a way that is somehow caring in a business that tells people, 'don't care; keep an arm's length.'

"In the Catholic Church, what the pope does isn't that important to me. I expect him to say stuff that is misguided or inconsequential. What's important to me is my parish and the people I see in church or our prayer group." When challenged on this congregational notion of Catholicism, Reardon offers a proviso:

"If it was just a local community without tradition, no, I wouldn't want that. But our parish is a community coming out of a tradition of believers around the world and going back thousands of years."

Reardon's early training provided a sense that there were critical matters of faith, largely unchanging, and also less consequential practices or customs.

"A lot of peripheral things like birth control or eating meat on Friday—those change," Reardon says, though pairing those two items as marginal might not jive with the Vatican's approach. What does not change for Reardon is the core of his belief and life: Jesus, love, redemption and a conviction that these translate into behavior.

So one challenge for writers of faith is to look for the faith or beliefs that motivate other people, both subjects and readers. For starters, Reardon thinks his work is the better for this insight.

"Generally, when I run into someone who is passionate about something, whether it's fixing the schools or cleaning up the water or helping people on welfare, I find it easier to believe that this someone has values, as compared to some other reporters who may think it is all a show to get and keep power.

"A big failing in journalism is that those in the business have a hard time seeing that people will do good. "

While reporters must be skeptical, he says, "you have to realize that people do act on their beliefs, in some, if not all, cases. And some people act more on beliefs than others. To rule that out and think everyone is acting for his or her own gain is to miss the point. If you have strong beliefs yourself, it is easier to accept that others do.

"Whenever I'm talking to someone or writing about a neighborhood, I'm looking for what values people bring in addition to what personal gain they have on line."

Reardon gives an example of a neighborhood that was trying to remain stable, at least economically, while it changed from an all-white to an integrated or largely black area. He was better off for knowing that "stable" was often a code word for "all-white," though not in this case.

Sometimes, people's values are closer to the surface. While researching a series of stories on efforts to rejuvenate the Chicago River, Reardon routinely heard "statements that had passion or poetry behind them." If a subject's beliefs do not emerge during reporting, he simply asks, "Why do you do this?"

A journalist or writer may find it hard to keep this respect for beliefs. The trade is populated, after all, by people whose high hopes for changing the world by telling the truth are constantly dashed.

"People get into the profession because they are idealistic," Reardon insists. "Then they get jaded because they run into people who say one thing and don't follow what they say." Sooner or later, many reporters learn not to believe in the professed ideals of others and simply stop asking about beliefs and values. Reardon hopes that younger reporters on the verge of terminal skepticism may be encouraged by his example.

"I hope that when they look at me, they see faith or belief or values as something I factor into the reporting when I am writing about a person or a neighborhood. I hope they see that there is more to people's values than personal gain."

Now comes a tougher matter for a devout reporter who realizes that most people act out of certain values and beliefs: Can she or he hold public figures and other subjects up against their professed beliefs?

"There is a complex interrelationship between what they believe, what they proclaim, and what they do. So much of what I write about goes to the 'why' of things: why is this neighborhood changing or why is this politician making this decision about the bank of the Chicago River? So you weigh actions against professed values. If people say, 'I love Chicago but I'm moving out,' I want to know why.

"You can't be a good reporter without going to the 'why' of things, and you can't get to 'why' without going to people's values. If they think personal gain is the most important thing, then they will act that way. Or maybe they have other values that counterbalance personal gain."

Sometimes a reporter has to overcome a prevailing belief, such as prejudice, in order to produce good work. "The positives of being in a mixed environment are often underplayed. There's a subtle way of thinking that newspapers buy into, namely that all white places are better than diverse ones or that all middle-class places are better than more economically diverse ones or that 'all-American' places are better than mixed ones."

Reardon finds his neighborhood, with people from the Philippines and Mississippi and Ireland and Pakistan, makes for "a pretty vibrant and lively kind of place."

He notes that some people are scared of diversity, due to "a societal message" that "you're safer in a lot of ways if you're in an area where you are with a lot of people like yourself."

But he cautions against hasty judgments. "It is a complex thing, and it is important for a reporter to say one group is not wrong because of a choice they made as to whether to live in the city or suburbs."

Do faith and values and a willingness to seek out those virtues in others shape an agenda for Reardon's work?

Yes and no.

"I'm trying to do stories that draw people together rather than drive them apart. Or if they are in a situation where they are being driven apart, I try to help them see that or make them understand their world and why things work the way they do. I want to do stuff that helps people make the right decisions."

Not that they always make those decisions. Reardon has written often that, although Chicago schools spend about the same per pupil as suburban schools, most of the students Chicago is trying to teach are from poor households and have various disadvantages. Despite his best efforts to expose and explain this inequity in print, Reardon remains frustrated by the absence of reform. "Even though I write about it frequently, there has been no groundswell to change school finance."

To be sure, readers are not eager to read only weighty articles that decipher social problems. Most newspapers and reporters try to serve up a variety of stories to entertain as well as inform.

"Sometimes readers want to read about something trivial, so I'll write that. Or they may need to read about something substantial, so I'll give that to them. And as for what I like to write about, I like to explain things."

So what is the purpose of a newspaper?

"To tell the truth," says Reardon without hesitation. Aside from the loftier goals of journalism, reporters of conscience are challenged daily to behave decently. Reardon has one advantage over most reporters, who generally are a whining lot.

"I don't grouse as much as I should. That may be from coming from a family of fourteen kids, where there wasn't much room for grousing. So I'm not good at that now. I look at other people, and sometimes I'm jealous that they're good at it and I'm not."

He also works to overcome the individualism of reporting by helping others track down U.S. census and historical data. He has a special interest in history and has written articles on such topics as the Haymarket Incident of 1886, Martin Luther King's "I Have a Dream" speech, and Jacob Riis, the nineteenth-century social reformer who photographed New York's poor and immigrant classes. He has been a member of an urban affairs group at the *Tribune* to figure out how to better cover and serve Chicago.

There are other on-the-job pitfalls. One is oversimplifying the news to make it fit a newspaper. A related danger is changing a story to please colleagues, especially editors, inappropriately.

"There is a simplification that takes place in newspapers to take a subject you spend weeks or months working on and reduce that subject to a small amount of space," Reardon warns. Simplification is one thing; oversimplification another.

"It's an art to know how to simplify, which nuances to leave in or which to leave out," he says. "Am I leaving this nuance in because editors will like it and give it better play?"

Once a story is done, reporters usually move on to the next topic. Subjects can feel abandoned. Reardon praises the approach of Alex Kotlowitz, the *Wall Street Journal* reporter who wrote a book about the life of one family in a Chicago housing project titled *There Are No Children Here*. Afterward, Kotlowitz stayed in touch with the family and used some of his book earnings to establish a college fund for the boys. "Often, as reporters we drop in and drop out of people's lives," says Reardon. "It's not that Kotlowitz adopted the family, but he stayed in touch."

Of course, some journalists eschew any personal attachment to the subject in an effort to remain impartial. That leaves Reardon uneasy.

"Journalism has developed objectivity to a degree where we're standing on the sidelines when we should step in and stop something. It's something I'm grappling with more and more—how to keep your distance in order to evaluate something and how to keep your humanity.

"I'm able to solve that dilemma most by being able to bring a certain weight to my writing. I can say things that carry some weight because I have the background. For instance, I know more about school funding than almost anyone else in Illinois. I have to be careful, but many times I can say stuff as a fact because I've written about it before."

He does reject the misrepresentation he saw among some old-timers at the City News Bureau, who would call relatives of a dead person and say they were from the coroner's office. And, while straightforward questions are the standard and reliable method, Reardon mentions a slightly more daring approach.

"I'm learning more now about the value of using open-ended questions to get people to say what they think, rather than what I need, for story. I am more and more aware of the richness that can result when you're not so direct." For instance, as part of his reporting for a series on the future of the

Faith in Words

Chicago River, Reardon realized that people have deep, visceral reactions to the waterway.

"I spent some mornings with kids and adults who were doing things around the river. With one class of students on a field trip, I just watched them, taking just two pages of notes for two hours of being out there. Yet I was able to bring into my story a sense of the river itself. I wasn't tipping them off to what I expected them to tell me."

He calls the approach "more speculative, because you don't know what you're getting out of it until later. It's another way of letting people express what's important, rather than just using them as quote machines."

Too often, he notes, a reporter needs an anecdote with which to start a feature story. What happens is that a reporter will seek out a compelling anecdote, get it in the first two minutes of talking to someone, and then "spend the next twenty minutes getting out of the interview."

Of course, being kind and deliberate requires the sort of time a cub reporter may not always have, especially when dealing with surly editors. But a little consideration is possible in the worst of circumstances—and it helps to open doors or keep people on the phone longer.

Reardon doesn't suspect that a person who reads this or that story of his would guess he is a person of faith and a reporter with high standards and strong values. "But if they read all of them, they would get that."

Being polite does not mean being cozy with newsmakers and their representatives. "I've really tried to keep an arm's length from sources by not going to lunch, fishing, ball games with them. I have felt real uncomfortable with that because how often does it then end up that you give them a pass on a story?"

He mentions a good friend who became a spokesman for a local university. When a controversy arose over the school's plan to evict an open-air market from their property, Reardon let others handle the story. Part of his motivation, he admits, was selfish. "I didn't want to write bad stuff about my friend's university."

Which reminds him of a related personal shortcoming. "One drawback in my reporting is I'm too nice to people. I have a hard time writing stuff they'll feel bad about. I do have to fight the tendency—and that's with people I don't know," Reardon adds with a laugh. To counter that tendency, he wants to take some risks with colleagues.

"Something that would be helpful to me as a person and as a reporter would be to get close to some people who share my values, to risk being vulnerable by exposing who I am more. There is such a strong thrust toward the suburbs, in the office and the city. As someone who loves the city and its ethnic diversity and architecture and its transportation opportunities and the lakefront and cultural opportunities, I can feel real isolated from people at the paper and in general. So I am seeking out people who share that mind-set."

He takes steps in his personal life to bolster, develop and maintain his faith and values. One is a prayer group of eleven years standing that he and his wife meet with every three weeks. However, many of the members live in the suburbs and aren't as passionate as he is about the city. Previously, the Reardons had a good experience with the Renew program in their parish, where they met one couple who became close friends. "A lot of it involved sharing our faith," he says.

He draws strength from his parish and the informal Mass held Sundays at 10:30 a.m. in St. Gertrude's school gym. Reardon expects little from the higher-ups in the Catholic Church. "I have been so disappointed with the hierarchy that I don't pay attention. I wish they would be leaders, be less politicians and more prophets."

Reardon wishes there were more opportunities to share

faith and strength, or at least a discussion, with reporters and editors at the newspaper. He says many colleagues are grappling with the central issues: "How to get at truth, how to deal with questions of values, how to work those in, and how to address them in your work." But more often than not, these are discussed briefly and usually in a rush.

Reardon believes burnout, an occupational hazard in journalism, can be avoided. "My wife and I and our kids live life full out, so burn-out is always a likelihood. What I'm doing is constantly feeling like I'm growing, and if you are always growing, you're not going to burn out. Or if you burn out in one area, you find a new one. Right now, I feel I'm still learning, and that's a way to not burn out.

"Learning is getting closer to the mystery of life. My mother always quoted Einstein, who said the more he knew, the more he realized what he didn't know. I don't know if he actually said that; it's what my mother said he said." Another leg of Reardon's personal maintenance program is a history book club he helped start. It meets every couple of months.

He does pray, though he avoids formula prayer. "I find my communications with God in my relationships with people, particularly my wife and kids, and in art, which includes literature, painting and music. I used to write poetry, and I would still like to get it published. It was part of trying to get at the mystery of life through words." Music, from Bob Dylan to Frank Sinatra to Rachmaninoff, provides another avenue.

"God speaks to me through the relationships I have with my friends and family—it is the mix of learning who they are and who I am through the way we are together."

Reardon also shared his faith, in a big way, through his 1995 book, *Daily Meditations (With Scripture) For Busy Dads.* He is convinced that the mundane can convey the Divine. "There was a moment when my son was three years old, and he ran one day through the house without his shirt on. Just the way his shoulder blades moved in his back was somehow pregnant with everything that is meaningful or with every answer in life. I'm always wrestling with these kinds of things to understand what they're saying, because what they're saying is somehow God talking."

How far will Patrick Reardon let his faith and values lead him?

"I know that what I'm doing is important and that what I bring to it is unique. I don't talk about that too much at work because that would scare the wits out of them. But a good reporter is a prophet, telling the truth."

Could he be led out of journalism? Not likely.

"The only thing I'd consider is whether there might be another type of writing, say books, that would be closer to getting at the mystery of who we are and what this is all about."

FIVE

Jan Larson

Journalism professor, writer, former editor and reporter

For Jan Larson—a devout Christian and Lutheran, journalism professor, writer and former editor and reporter—doing good work is a response to salvation rather than a way of earning it.

"While I do not believe that there are good works that save me, I do believe that in response to Christ and the gift of life that he gave us on the cross I want my life and actions to be a good reflection of my faith. Little children respond to love positively, so what should my response be to the ultimate love except something good?

"I don't know that good works are an everyday occurence," she admits. "It is hard to think of covering a city council meeting as doing something for Christ, but if you are doing the best you can to provide your readers with information they need to make decisions, then maybe that is giving glory to God because you are not being lazy. That's part of being a Christian, that you do not settle for 'good enough' but are always striving for excellence."

Practicing her beliefs is not always easy. Sometimes it costs when a reporter's spirituality comes into play. When Larson was an assistant city editor in Ithaca, New York, a single mother was murdered. Larson and her staff followed the story as police sought a suspect. The woman left behind a daughter and her own mother.

"The woman's mother called and asked if we were going to be writing a story. I said yes, and my editor overheard and wanted me to conduct an interview because I had the victim's mother on the line. But the mother became close to hysterical as we talked, so I told her we would want to interview her at some other time. I could not, morally, interview her then since she was too upset. At the same time, my editor was getting increasingly angry with me. I told the woman I was praying for her and I was sorry for her loss and I let her go. The editor hassled me a lot about letting her go without getting something, but I said I made a decision I knew to be correct."

It was just such editorial values that propelled Larson out of the newsroom. "I got into teaching partly because of the newsroom environment. It's hard being surrounded by so many cynics."

And Larson has the courage of her convictions. She is a direct woman, with dark hair and eyes, and with high expectations for herself and others. She looks straight at you, making you feel cherished and challenged simultaneously. She is one of those clear and uncluttered people who can make an interviewer uncomfortably aware of self-deception and half-hearted efforts. In her presence, one is not inclined to fudge the truth or make false assertions.

Today she is an associate professor in the Department of Communication and Journalism at the University of Wisconsin-Eau Claire. She lives in Eau Claire with her engineer husband, Lauran, and their three children, Grey, Ellie and Dana. She is a contributing writer for *American Demographics* magazine. Her career in newspapers included stints as a business editor and assistant city editor at the *Ithaca Journal*, an education reporter at the *Anchorage Times*, and columnist and reporter at the *Peninsula Clarion* in Kenai, Alaska. The decision to leave the newsroom has been good for her family and has also enabled Larson to live her faith.

"Lauran was very glad to have me out of the newsroom. He felt I came home every day and told him all the bad news of the world. From my own experience, I knew it would be nice to teach and to pass on what I had learned. As I had developed a family life, teaching provided an opportunity for that."

Rather than having to discover a faith as an adult, Larson grew up with one that still fits—with some adjustments.

"My father was for many years a Lutheran lay minister and then a pastor, so religion was like breathing. I have a very simple faith. I never questioned the fact that Jesus Christ is the Son of God and that he died for me. That's just something I know—Baptism worked! And my faith has always been a part of who I am, even though there were times in my life when I didn't acknowledge it much."

Her childhood granted her another gift: sensitivity to cross-cultural and economic issues. Larson was born Jan Mireles. Her father is of Hispanic background and her mother of Danish extraction. Living on a minister's salary, her family did not live in luxury, but Larson did acquire other goods.

"My dad is always saying he didn't give us kids enough. I'm always telling him that what he and Mom gave us was more important."

How does her faith translate into a code she can carry through her day?

"Well, there are the Ten Commandments. A code of personal ethics is something I stress to my students, though it is hard in a state school to discuss religion. I tell them to develop their own values and keep them, despite pressure from editors and colleagues. They have to live with themselves and they have to go home at night and sleep with themselves."

Larson lets her students know she is a Christian. Rather than being overtly religious, she offers philosophical models to budding journalists, such as Aristotle's golden mean or John Mill's principles of utilitarianism. She is aware that living according to one's beliefs can easily be pulverized by the juggernaut of deadlines and screaming editors and the excitement of a news scoop.

"It basically comes down to a philosophical decision. Where do your loyalties lie: with your readers, yourself, your publication, or is it a mixture? The students need this question reinforced every class. They hear it in one class and it's gone from the brain. I may not agree with what decision they turn to, but as long as it's consistent I'm satisfied."

She also tells students to do what she tried as a journalist. "I encourage them to get a dialogue on these issues going in their newsroom."

As a journalist and teacher, Larson goes further and seeks out fellow Christians for personal support and help. Having beliefs of her own makes her sensitive to those of others.

"When people are grieving or are attached to a certain issue, I want to be able to be sensitive to those things, because I would want them to respect mine. I have lived with this innate sense that I have my beliefs and you have yours."

Having developed her daily code of behavior, can a journalist have an agenda for the stories she pursues?

Larson notes that the mere idea of an agenda "does have a negative connotation," but she is not entirely uncomfortable with the idea. First, she recalls her time as a business editor.

"When I started that job, I had no clue what I was doing, but I turned the business page into a page I would want to read as a woman. I brought in day-care issues, women in the workplace, and just expanded the focus of that page.

"We all have our personal biases, and we cannot escape them. They shape the way we think and write. To say unbiased reporting is the norm is false; what's important is to be aware of your biases. To some degree, who I am as a Christian definitely shapes my work. There are times I have to set aside or at least try to distance myself from my beliefs to report a story fairly. For example, say I am opposed to abortion and I'm assigned to cover what the popular press calls a 'pro-choice' rally. I go and listen and offer respect and report on it. That's my job."

But the work doesn't stop there. Whether a pro-life or a pro-choice rally, a reporter with strong feelings on the topic should scrutinize the facts.

"If their information is wrong, I will point that out," Larson relates. "My students went to cover a pro-choice rally and they came back with a pamphlet with incorrect statistics, which they used in their reporting. I told them they had to double-check these things."

As any good reporter or editor knows, the best stories often spring from personal beliefs or interests. While at Columbia University's Graduate School of Journalism, Larson studied New York City's annual report of health statistics. Deep in the tangle of charts and tables, she noticed an interesting fact about abortions in New York—that most were being had by women who were single, prosperous, and often white.

"That's also part of developing my personal position against abortion," Larson explains. "I saw those statistics and I said, 'Wait a minute.' They always say it is poor women and victims of rape or incest, but I realized it is more often women with jobs who don't want to be inconvenienced."

Without advancing any particular side, Larson had spotted a genuinely good story, thanks to her own feelings on the subject. Practicing her religion tipped her off to another story, one she wrote for *American Demographics* on the greying of the Protestant church. She had seen it happening in the aisles around her, something a reporter who'd never darkened a church or synagogue doorway would not notice.

A better venue for deploying her religious beliefs came in her columns, "because that was me and it was where I could approach sensitive issues from the perspective of a Christian." Larson gives a few examples from her days in Alaska.

"One Christmas I bemoaned in one of my columns that once again I had not prepared spiritually for the birth of Christ. I was working in a small town and people approached me on the street, everywhere. I had a rough-and-tumble oil worker come up to me in this little restaurant; he stood looming over the table and thanked me, because he felt that way too and didn't know how to get past it."

In another column, Larson wrote about death and tragedy. "I had covered a plane crash in which all nine people were burned to death. The firefighters had to go out there and extinguish burning bodies. It was terribly traumatic for them and the whole community. I wrote about that from a Christian perspective, expressing sorrow for the families and gratitude to the firefighters."

She said many thanked her for the column, notably one firefighter who found it hard to read but important and helpful. Such efforts run against the prevailing ethic of newsrooms, which foster an almost macho sense that the best reporters never, ever let their feelings interfere with their telling the hard, cold facts.

"As journalists, we had it hammered into us that we weren't important," notes Larson, "that who we were should be invisible to readers. When I was younger, I never wanted my opinion in stories; as I matured, I realized that is impossible. Who I am shapes whom I choose to interview, what facts I decide are relevant, how I arrange them in a story."

The process of reporting, which puts a writer in contact with some of life's less pleasant characters as well as into stressful situations, calls for careful execution of one's beliefs.

"You can always treat people with respect," says Larson. "There is no excuse for not having good manners. It's the lessons you learned at home from Mom and Dad: Be polite, say please, no matter who you are dealing with. That does not mean you are not honest or straightforward with readers. You do not cover something up because it will be unpleasant to read or difficult for the subject."

Many reporters balance carefully their need for information with their responsibility to be honest and fair. If a source clams up, there goes the story.

"You have to get them to like you to have them talk to you," Larson admits. While not one to shy away from confrontation, Larson says she realizes that "you have to be an open person and realize you are taking a lot. Every chance you have to give, you should. Sometimes sharing a little of myself in the interview helps. If somebody needs a bit of my time to explain something I'm not going to use, I listen. But I will try to redirect the conversation into more fruitful waters, to mix my metaphors."

Larson admits ruefully she has seen, and been, "the sort of idiot reporter who bangs on the door and says 'Give me what I want.'" But stopping, listening and giving of herself and her time has led to marvelous encounters with people and invariably made for a better story, she says.

Coming from an Anglo and Hispanic background makes Larson more sensitive to the issue of multiethnic, multiracial children, which helped with one article she wrote on the subject.

"Many people want the U.S. census to list them as multi-racial. Say Mom is white and Dad is black. The government classifies you by your mom's race, which is white. But the school lists you by sight, say, as black. But you say, 'I'm white.'

"With everyone I talked to for that story, I spoke of my own family—my mother is white and my dad is Hispanic—and that at times had been difficult for us growing up. With one woman I interviewed, my background was important. She was white and had black children, and she could see that I could relate to what she and her family were experiencing."

Opening up also reinforces a writer's duty to be fair. "Sometimes by sharing ourselves, we can establish more trust and credibility and it holds us more accountable," Larson says. "We realize they have trusted us with sensitive information, so we are more inclined to treat that information with respect and will not toss it out."

Writing and reporting are hard when one wants to behave with fairness and compassion. Does Larson's faith give her the courage she needs in her daily work and life?

"Certainly," she responds. "Human beings are basically weak, and left to our own devices we are going to sink to the lowest level. My faith enables me to act, at the very least, decently." She also asks for help in situations where she is afraid, such as attending a news conference as a college student with the former mayor of New York City, Ed Koch.

"He's an intimidating guy. In situations like that I'll say a little prayer, 'Okay God, hold me up.' When I have trouble writing a story, it's so liberating. I write my little outline, I say my little prayer, and I get through it."

Could an observer or a reader discern that Larson is a Christian?

"I would like to think so, but I don't know. I try to end all my interviews on a pleasant note, so the other person feels the time spent with me was worthwhile. It's not always possible, especially in those adversarial relations reporters often have, but I want them to feel 'at least she wasn't out to get me and I had my say.'"

Larson's values have also enabled her to pull back on a story or change its focus despite outside pressures to deliver the original premise. "I wouldn't twist things to meet a deadline or please an editor."

Then there are the financial pressures. Low salaries and stiff competition for advancement drive many idealistic reporters out of the news business.

"If somebody told me in college I would be destitute as a reporter, then maybe I would not have gone into it," Larson says, later adding that she never went into the business thinking of money. "There are always other things out there I can do to earn money. I always want to be in reporting or writing to some extent. I grew up in a large family without a lot of money, and though we have more than ever due to my husband's work we are trying to make people and activities the focus of our life, not money. I realized long ago that money doesn't guarantee happiness. It's often a trap. Financial security can be a trap."

At the same time, Larson says she has become cannier about negotiating compensation with employers. As a cub reporter, she would settle for any salary. As she became confident of her worth, Larson began asking for a certain amount before being hired.

Another professional liability is loneliness. Though it strikes many a reporter in a crowded newsroom, isolation can overwhelm a freelancer working from home.

"I remember sitting at my desk staring out the window, waiting for my husband to get home, and desperate for human contact other than over the phone line. You have to build in contacts with other people to combat loneliness, whether with a spouse or friend. You have to take extraordinary steps to get outside the job."

In Kenai, Alaska, Larson was involved in community theater, "to meet other people and be known as something other than just that reporter who's always causing trouble." She also seeks out colleagues who share her Christian beliefs, which may require being public—in word or action—about those beliefs.

Faith in Words

"You have to be willing to tell people what you believe in or they won't know. Religion is one thing journalists are afraid of.

"I wait until they get to know me as a person and as a Christian. I have had some friends start going to church as a result of our conversations. One saw a difference in me because of my religion." Then, with some false annoyance in her tone, Larson adds, "She started going to a Lutheran church, but not mine!"

A daily spiritual discipline, even the slightest, keeps Larson on the beam.

"Oh, I'm bad; usually first just prayers. One of my goals is to have daily Bible time. I'll pray at different times during the day, as people cross my mind, but nothing organized. On Sunday we go to church, where we are active as lay ministers."

As have many churches and parishes, Larson's congregation has created small groups to personalize the community. "We keep tabs with each other and our needs. Several years ago we worked with Habitat for Humanity, now we're with other organizations. There are six or seven of of us, and it's a mix of fellowship, Bible study and socializing. We meet twice a month."

The Larsons have also worked in their church's drama ministry and taught Sunday school. Her fellow Lutherans often help with her professional struggles. She talks to her husband or her pastor or submits requests to a prayer chain the congregation formed.

Does it help? "Prayer always helps," Larson says emphatically. "Things have improved tremendously at work over the last year. I have a lot of new colleagues and there was a difficult merger with another department. My attitude is improving."

The last remark raises for Larson the truism that we do indeed make the world after our own image.

"If we decide to be happy people, we will be. I have days when all goes well. And there are times when I just fall apart."

Counting her blessings always helps. Most of all, so does her faith.

"I do seriously wonder how people are happy without God in their lives. We need God desperately. He's what gets me through."

SIX

David Scott

Editor, Our Sunday Visitor

Ask David Scott how he landed first in upstate New York and then in Indiana, writing and editing stories on such topics as prominent Catholic women, the future of the Church, and prayer in the modern era, and he will tell you about a woman at a bus stop.

"In college, I studied Marxism and communications theory, and I saw religion as a crutch," says Scott, editor of *Our Sunday Visitor*, a national Catholic weekly published in Huntington, Indiana. With a circulation of about ninety thousand, it is the largest national Catholic newspaper. Scott was previously assistant editor of *The Evangelist*, the weekly newspaper of the Albany (New York) Diocese.

After graduating from Boston University in 1983, Scott moved to Washington, D.C. on a legislative fellowship. He worked on Capitol Hill for nine months, then took a high-paying job as a writer with a telecommunications publication. He lived in the Mount Pleasant neighborhood, where Latin American immigrants rub shoulders with American blacks, affluent professionals, and blue-collar workers. Despite his academically honed skepticism, Scott was impressed by the religious faith of many of his neighbors. One mother, busy with her family and shopping, steered Scott back to the Bible and the faith of his parents by mere example.

"There was one woman who used to wait for the bus with her three kids and several heavy bags of groceries," he remembers. "And she was always praying the rosary."

Seeing her and others, deeply faithful though not rich in the eyes of the world, "got me back reading the Bible," says Scott, who was baptized and raised Catholic by his parents in Avon, Connecticut.

The knock on the door came a second time at Revolution Books, a nearby center for Marxist and other literature.

"I saw a copy of *A Theology of Liberation* by Gustavo Guttierez. The cover caught my eye: a sculpture of an agonized Christ," Scott recalls. The image reminded him of God's love for the poor, the sort of people he was living with in Mount Pleasant. Here was the God of the lady at the bus stop.

In 1985, Scott married a devout Catholic, which led him to consider his own faith more deeply. He began attending Mass again and decided to study religion. He received a master's degree from Pittsburgh Theological Seminary. "It was the most affordable place I could find for graduate studies," he says.

In October 1989, Scott was hired by *The Evangelist* in Albany, a newspaper with a circulation of about sixty thousand in a diocese the size of Massachusetts, extending from the historic Hudson Valley north to the remote towns of the Adirondacks. Readers include working-class and ethnic conservatives, educated middle-class civil servants and professionals, and sophisticated teachers, writers and artists. The diocese is headed by thoughtfully progressive Bishop Howard Hubbard. Albany's Catholics are assertive in church matters and active in social justice and peace issues.

Hubbard is the newspaper's publisher, though his role is a distant one, since he and the editor are of one mind on the paper's direction and purpose. As with most of the Catholic press, the average reader is more likely to be over sixty than under forty. *The Evangelist* is larger than papers in comparable dioceses because a good portion of its revenues comes from running legal advertisements for the city of Albany. Here, what had been purely cerebral for Scott bore spiritual fruit.

"When we moved here, I started attending daily Mass, if only for the order and habit," he said. "But somewhere along the line, it became not just an intellectual exercise but something I wanted for my life."

In that job and later at *Our Sunday Visitor*, Scott was able to combine his love of writing and editing with his re-christened religious beliefs to provide a basis for his day-to-day moral code.

"I was never uncomfortable with journalism as advocacy," he says. "My first real hero was George Orwell, not so much for his novels, but for his writing in *The Road to Wigan Pier* and *Down and Out in London and Paris*," two nonfiction accounts of the lives of people in poor communities. Muckraking journalist I.F. Stone is another hero and role model.

For discernment and rejuvenation, Scott tries to pray every day. "I pray to Joseph and Mary for help in parenting and being a spouse. In terms of my craft, I have my icons." He points to a picture of Dorothy Day on the bulletin board over his desk. Journalist and co-founder of the Catholic Worker Movement, Day exhibited qualities in her life that most writers envy: the wisdom to see the world's tricks and tragedies clearly and without sentiment; compassion rooted in a sure sense of one's values and role; and an eagerness to know more fully men and women, their works, and their aspirations.

Though he used to pray to Saint Francis de Sales, patron of newspaper reporters, Scott turned to Day "in terms of people I want to side with: the poor, the less fortunate, people whose voices don't get heard."

Given his own strong religious beliefs, how does Scott know whether or not the people he writes about and for have equally strong spiritual lives?

"I start with the assumption that everyone is telling me the truth," he says. Then, working for a Catholic publication, topics are more apt to be religious. His work allows him to dip into a deep reservoir that most journalists overlook. He has been struck by the faith of the poor and disadvantaged, those who have the least but believe the most.

"This summer I interviewed about two dozen homeless persons," he relates. "I asked them, 'Do you find it hard to believe in God when you don't have a house or good food and clothing?' It was easy to ask. People are dying to talk about God, since no one ever asks them."

Religious writers are not the only reporters who can explore such questions. Scott notes that reporters for daily newspapers, when looking for local reaction to national or international events, resort to the same tired round of experts.

"When there's a national issue they want to localize, newspapers ask the usual suspects and call academics, teachers, local politicians," he says. "They don't call religious leaders unless it's a religious issue." But considering polls showing that most Americans regularly attend worship services, Scott believes the secular media should wake up to the possibilities.

"Why not ask Bishop Hubbard about free trade with Mexico, how it might effect the social compact here and what we owe a poorer nation?" he asks. "Or ask pastors what their parishioners think about the invasion of Panama or the war on drugs."

During the war with Iraq, many newspapers showed photographs of people praying for peace, but it remained, Scott says, a flat and misleading image.

"The pictures showed one dimension, as if to say 'they thought it all out and now they're praying.' And it seemed as if people were praying out of weakness, not strength. But for many of us, it's not 'I've thought it all out and now God will help me' but 'I'll pray first because that's what I do, and then I'll ask for guidance.'"

But recognizing that others have spiritual lives does not necessarily give an editor or reporter the right to judge. "It's not my job to see if people are hypocrites," Scott says, then reconsiders. "Well, I did it with Bush, but he opened himself up to it by calling the Persian Gulf War a just one, so I wrote a couple of articles on what is a just war and whether this was one." With his current job, however, Scott feels more comfortable explicating the Church's teachings.

"The goal I have with *Our Sunday Visitor*, my vocation as a Catholic journalist, is to present people with a Catholic vision of life, to attract people close to the person of Christ who is revealed in the Church, to help them live out their faith and eventually get to heaven."

Scott agrees that a journalist is called to hold up public officials to scrutiny. He wishes the Catholic press did a better job with religious leaders. When a bishop retires after being accused of having an affair, for example, a few paragraphs in the diocesan paper about how the entire church suffers is not enough.

"That's not going to help anyone," Scott says vehemently. "The major criticism of the Catholic press is that it has a too-rosy view of the world."

Still, he admits a reluctance to judge anyone in print. "Two things hit me about Jesus in Scripture: 'judge not,' and we should 'forgive seven times seventy.'"

Scott is hard on his professional colleagues. For one thing, he wishes they would present more clearly and thoroughly Church teachings on controversial issues such as birth control, clerical celibacy, women's ordination, homosexuality, and papal authority. Too often, as in the mainstream media, the conflict gets the ink rather than the cause of the conflict.

"What annoys me is that many Catholic newspapers have neither the knowledge nor the true belief in these teachings to proclaim them to their readers; hence, there's much confusion among Catholics, a situation that is a shame and a scandal."

Scott admits that keeping to his personal agenda may be easier as an editor of a Catholic newspaper than at a secular periodical.

"The job is defined as social justice, the parameters are laid out in Matthew 25: to cover the hungry, the poor, the sick—the people with whom Jesus identified himself. I try to make sure people know what the social justice issues are. Those are the categories I try to stick to."

Watching Scott at work, would anyone know he is a Christian? He struggles with the question. Sometimes rudeness is built into the job.

"I try to be real kind. I know most people are not comfortable with reporters. I may blow in to a welfare hearing for half an hour with a photographer, and that's not going to leave a good impression," he admits. Out of basic fairness, he sends most subjects a copy of the published article, which is far more than the vast majority of journalists do.

"I don't know how to do my job so people know I am a Christian. I try to be nice, but that's courtesy. I don't know if it's faith."

Though a clear and versatile thinker, Scott found reflecting on the connection between his spiritual life and his work a challenge. Like many journalists, he does not stop every day to explore his deeper motives, but he obviously lives on the basis of faith. He has his beliefs, sets his compass thus, and his life unfolds accordingly.

It would be hard to picture him being rude or hardnosed. Of medium height and balding, his round face is ringed by a beard and often tilts to one side as he ponders a question. Before he speaks, he exhales softly, stretching out the first syllable of a reply as if he wants to consider his answer just one more second while not keeping a listener waiting.

Scott tries to forgo the knee-jerk aggressive posture of many reporters and focus on a constructive role, though not one he sacrifices to boosterism.

"I remember learning journalism as an attack mode. I try to build people up; I'm not looking for hypocrites. A lot of people don't realize what a difference they're making.

"I try to make sure my writing is charitable. Not in a namby-pamby sense, but I never want to treat someone without the dignity they're born with. In Albany, I did that once with a homeless woman who was quite fat and not very clean. I described her accurately but without charity."

Scott said *The Evangelist*'s editor called him on it and the realization stung. "I should have stuck more to the facts and less to judging. People who write for the *New York Times* metropolitan section do an amazing job of describing someone without crossing the line."

Scott stretched the boundaries of *The Evangelist*'s coverage beyond the regular round of parish prayer groups, announcements from the bishops, and the latest church anniversary. The example is a good one for other diocesan weeklies, which often avoid hard news. His front page analysis article in May 1993 untangled the issues behind the Bosnian War in a series of simply worded questions and answers. Scott proceeded from "What's going on in Bosnia? How did the conflict start?" to reasons for and against armed intervention. In the last section, he tackled the stickiest issues: America's hoary notions of Balkan history and the convenient theory that violence is inevitable among these far-off and inscrutable peoples.

"It seems inaccurate and dangerous to accept the conventional wisdom that Bosnia is a case of an ancient clan or tribal warfare," he argued. "Croats, Slavs, Muslims and Serbs are not the barbaric, blood-spilling vampires depicted in the press; they are Europeans with a long and illustrious culture.

"The danger of looking at Bosnia as an ancient blood feud is that it casts the conflict as somehow inevitable, a destiny that can't be changed. As Pope John Paul II has said, war is not inevitable but is the result of sin, 'of greed for power, of the desire to dominate others, and of failure to respect their rights.'"

Scott noted that poverty and hopelessness fed the conflict, and that Catholics cannot look the other way when some part of humanity, "united in the Mystical Body of Christ," is being violated. He warned that the black-and-white thinking left over among many conservatives from the Cold War is no longer valid, and the fatalism and anti-Americanism of many liberals was of equally little use.

"Any intervention in Bosnia should not be about taking sides or choosing enemies to be destroyed. Any intervention should be on the side of the suffering people." Scott's analysis was remarkable for its ambition and depth. It was a challenge for readers to think and reflect and act.

At *Our Sunday Visitor*, Scott often lays aside the blue pencil to pen editorials and articles. An October 1996 editorial on the "The Soccer-Mom Nation" noted the "swift suburbanization of American political life, the takeover of politics by the people who have plenty." Another decried how a media-created hysteria over a "false crisis of priestly pedophiliacs" distracted attention from actual cases, from victims, and from treating the same perversion in the wider society. A July Fourth editorial lamented that, thanks to our individualism, "all Americans are infected to some degree by a disordered notion of freedom."

Though much of his time was spent editing at *The Evangelist*, Scott did a series profiling prominent Catholic women of the twentieth century, ranging from Dorothy Day to Edith Stein (a German Jew who converted to Catholicism, became a well-known Carmelite nun, and later died at Auschwitz) to

Catherine de Hueck Doherty (who worked with the poor in Harlem and later founded Madonna House, a center for religious renewal in rural Canada). The articles combined historical research with contemporary reevaluation, if necessary, and examples of what these women may mean to modern readers. Scott saw the series as a means to redress some of the neglect women still suffer in the Church.

Scott's first-person accounts on the problems facing farmers beset by suburban development, rising taxes, and sluggish food prices combined trenchant economic and moral insights and lifted the articles above the normal "Old MacDonald" fare some newspapers deliver in their occasional agricultural reporting.

At *The Evangelist*, Scott also explored the ramifications of materialism in America and in the Albany area. Not afraid to tackle the big issues, he wrote a series on prayer and, during Lent, one on virtue and sin. In articles for the Washington Report on Middle East Affairs, he detailed the differing responses of the Vatican and the American bishops to the Persian Gulf War. Interestingly, he found Rome much harsher in its criticism while many in the United States' hierarchy rushed to defend the bombings as just.

Tackling the difficult issues furthers Scott's spiritual life and gives him the courage to continue in his occupation. One homeless woman, he says, "had the most faith content of anyone despite her circumstances. But she was realistic. She told me, 'I know there's a God but I don't think he's been looking on me for a long time.'"

Especially in such a complex case, Scott said, the need is even greater to depict "with charity" so that readers will see the truth beyond the facts. "The depth of her suffering was such that people might miss her faith and just see some beastly woman."

Scott realizes that a good journalist cannot always work on subjects he or she finds personally fulfilling, but the final story has to serve the readers.

"I don't care about how a parish council works, but I remind myself that it is important to those people and to the administration of churches. And there are priests who don't want to relinquish control, which is interesting. So I don't get excited, but I do try to do a good job. Even if I'm bored, I have an obligation to take the topics seriously."

Scott reads the work of other professionals as instructional texts, and he relies on simple good effort. "I read good journalists critically and see how they do it. And I do care what people think when they read the paper, so I try to write the best story I can."

Scott pauses. As a member of a profession that considers cynicism a high virtue, he appears embarrassed by his positivist tone. "When this stuff comes out of my mouth, I feel like Norman Vincent Peale."

Just as journalists for secular publications try to explain the world to their readers, so Scott sees his work as one of explaining Catholicism to his readers.

"As Catholics, we don't hear enough about making the Church teachings real. Birth control and celibacy have not been made clear to many Catholics. I've been through Catholic education, I've had formal training, and I don't understand them. There's a failure of the Church to explain things from the pulpit."

The Catholic press, even as in-house organs, can step into the breach. Pope Paul VI's encyclical, *Humanae Vitae*, is one example.

"I've read through the document, and there is the argument that, in the end, birth control will be used to weed out poor populations. And when you look at the history of birth control in this country, that's who it's aimed at. Now you see inner-city girls in Baltimore being given Norplant."

Scott strives to flesh out explanations of encyclicals and pastoral letters. Speaking shortly after he was hired by

Our Sunday Visitor, he recalled the national weekly had criticized President Bill Clinton's economic plan. The paper printed excerpts from Pope John Paul II's encyclical on the economy, *Centesimus Annus,* detailing the limits of state-run economies, with the collapse of Communism as proof.

In *The Evangelist*'s coverage of the issue, "I also pulled out excerpts on how capitalism failed to provide for everyone," says Scott. "The Church and the encyclicals are very large. There is room for all points of view."

In what may discomfort modern Catholics who support the welfare state, Scott reminded readers of *Our Sunday Visitor* in a review of a movie on Dorothy Day's life that this saintly woman, who dedicated herself to the poor, also vigorously opposed the New Deal. Why? It would, she said, "only engorge an already bloated state, dehumanize the poor, and inoculate average believers from their Christian duty to serve the poor personally and with sacrifice."

The hectic life of a journalist can make the most devout forget their spiritual basis. In the world of the Catholic press, the source of all life is easily left out. "Sometimes we get into these debates, and we forget God is up there. I can go through a whole week and not use the word *Jesus.*"

For practice, Scott spent a week at *The Evangelist* mentioning Jesus in every story, especially those concerning issues of social justice. His subjects were not on the same wavelength.

"I found people appealing to all sorts of things without mentioning Jesus. Even I find it easier to quote the encyclicals than Scripture. Jesus didn't know what the nuclear bomb was."

Or did he?

"Well, he didn't speak to the issue."

Scott keeps in touch with his beliefs by talking with like-minded colleagues. In the Albany Diocesan Pastoral Center, where *The Evangelist* was quartered, he was near other Catholics eager to do the Lord's work. But he had to reach beyond the newspaper. He and his boss were not close, and the reporters he supervised were not necessarily devout or learned in matters of doctrine and religion.

"Two of the women at the paper grilled me on Catholic teachings," says Scott, an exercise he found challenging but rewarding. "I worked with the younger writers, but they were more secular in their outlook. There were a couple of guys in the building I did talk faith with. It is nice to feel you are not alone."

In recent years, Scott has become more disciplined in his prayer and ascetic practice, with daily Mass, Scripture readings, the rosary, and regular confession. He is in good company at *Our Sunday Visitor*. He is less surrounded by cynics and he counts his editor-in-chief, Greg Erlandson, and his publisher, Bob Lockwood, as part of "a small core of folks here that I can talk with about faith and family and work."

In either a sign of approaching middle age or spiritual growth, Scott reports that he spends less time these days hashing out Church and political issues and more time discussing family, marriage and moral matters. He also fears seeming pious.

"I struggle every day with cynicism and with the sense that politics and culture are decadent and untethered to any moral core. I struggle hard with the stress of putting out a twenty-page edition every week, and I struggle hard to be a 'Christian' in my dealings with freelance writers, correspondents and my staff. I try hard, I fail often, I try again. Regular confession has become a big help. It is still a struggle to balance faith and work and family."

Of course, mundane chores can get in the way of the search of truth. "With kids now, I have less time. The hard part is finding God in silly moments or when I'm changing diapers." He smiles. "It is easier to find inspiration in the quiet moments, in books."

All talk and intents aside, many well-meaning writers find themselves sidetracked from—or shoved out of—their profession by the low pay. For those who have not taken a formal vow of poverty, supporting a family or oneself on a reporter's salary can mean peanut-butter sandwich lunches and spaghetti dinners for years. It can mean driving a ten-year-old car that breaks down monthly or not being able to give a son or daughter that special Christmas gift.

Scott and his wife, Sarah, have three girls and a boy. Before the children arrived, they agreed she would stay home to raise them, even though the decision meant foregoing one salary. As sole supporter, Scott knows what it is like to be pinched—even more so since he was spoiled by a good salary early on.

"At the age of twenty-five, I was earning forty-two thousand dollars a year. If I did corporate writing now, I could earn that or better and go home after work and have a martini instead of sitting down to write another freelance article. But then I would want to hang myself."

At *The Evangelist*, Scott would spend forty-five hours a week at the office, then another twenty or thirty on freelance work to make ends meet. He knows other journalists are under the same pressures. He helps younger reporters to know when a story they've written can be expanded and sold to an outside publication. He recommends markets and ideas, and offers advice on writing and construction.

But juggling work and family is a part of all marriages. "The plus side is that the kids will grow up with a work ethic, and with a good mother who is always there. Yes, I should be giving them more baths, but we talked about this before we decided Sarah would stay home."

Though freelancing is no longer necessary, his hours are long and Scott still worries that he spends too much time "winning bread" and not enough time just hanging out with his children. Yet, he confesses, "in the last few years I have felt closer to Christ and to my wife and children and experienced a clearer sense of God's direction and tender mercies in my life."

With Michael Aquilina, Scott has edited a book, *Weapons of the Spirit: Living a Holy Life in Unholy Times*, a selection of writings from Father John Hugo, pacifist, mystic and spiritual director of Dorothy Day. The two are working on another book, a selection of writings from Christianity's first millennium. And Scott is preparing a third volume, meditations on the Eucharist by Pope John Paul II.

In his job, Scott feels able to fulfill a longtime, heartfelt goal: "To proclaim Church teaching confidently, to offer it as a way of life that can be lived and is being lived by millions of people, even in the face of carping by many within the Church and despite the attacks on the Church by an aggressively secular culture, and remembering always that believers in places like China, Algeria, and even the United States are facing persecution and martyrdom as real as that faced by the first Christians in Rome."

SEVEN

Alan Abbey

Business editor, Albany Times-Union, former investigative reporter

God, some people say, gets our attention in different ways.

In 1987, Alan Abbey was hiking in the mountains of Nepal when he wandered away from his party, fell off a cliff, and broke both arms. It was the beginning of a slow but steady spiritual journey from the secular, middle-class Judaism of his youth to making religious observance the center of his life.

Abbey wandered alone for a day, with his arms dangling at his sides, before finding his party. He hiked several more days to a hospital in Katmandu, where medical care was superficial and his arms were set inadequately. He arrived home on Long Island with nerve damage, infections and other complications. Four operations and a long recuperation followed over the course of a year.

"From then, it was a significant journey both physically and emotionally to just get back to simply being able to walk around," says Abbey. "I was between jobs. It was a low point professionally, emotionally and spiritually."

Not that the sun broke through the clouds dramatically that one afternoon, but his adventure accelerated a longer journey that was already under way.

"When I went to Nepal, I brought an English language version of the Jewish Bible with me. I didn't read it over there, and I'm not sure what compelled me to buy it." Back home, he says, "there was no blinding moment, but over a period I began rethinking certain things."

Abbey is a tall, conservatively dressed, attentive man with brown hair and the sort of small square-framed glasses one sees on patrons at coffee bars. He fears many people think him straitlaced, despite his guitar-playing, iconoclasm, and vow to avoid growing up. After several years covering banks and finance, he was promoted to business editor of the Albany *Times Union*. To his work, Abbey brings a healthy cynicism about his profession and its exaggerated notions of self-importance and about the hidden agendas of business leaders and politicians.

He first entered journalism to overcome shyness and to fulfill a broad curiosity. After recovering from his accident, Abbey returned to newspaper work in 1987. But then, at age thirty-three, "I started feeling a greater need for family and community."

A friend led him back to Judaism's door.

"I was raised the way many mainstream American Jews are," he explains. "We observed many holidays; I was bar mitzvahed. Jewish awareness was always important but observance was not. Belief and religion were not discussed or made a part of daily life. And we didn't practice the basic Sabbath observances, which are at the core of Judaism."

In 1990, Abbey spent a Saturday with a woman "who showed me my lack of knowledge and the nice things that come from having knowledge." Observing the Sabbath with her gave Abbey "this realization that you are part of something bigger than yourself. We didn't go to the malls as everyone in New Jersey did; we spent this lovely spring day walking around the streets." Years later, the recollected calm of that Sabbath spreads across Abbey's face. "I was at peace, it was a very peaceful day."

The Sabbath, in concept and practice, he says, "even

more so than monotheism, may be the most important contribution of Judaism to the world. The awareness that life and people are cyclical, that there are times for resting and sitting back and taking things as opposed to trying to make things."

Though he was not aware of it at the time, the deeper message of that day's practice—as with the best of religious rituals and observances—continued to shape Abbey's spiritual life. The education accelerated later that year during three weeks' volunteer work in Israel, when Abbey felt a primeval unity with all Jews.

"It was a phenomenal experience, emotionally as well as educationally. I was there for the opening shots of the Gulf War, Iraq's invasion of Kuwait, when the entire country went into alert. I felt a sense of solidarity with the people that was just overwhelming. I certainly felt that their fate was inextricably intertwined with mine."

While there, he began eating kosher food, the only kind served at the Israel Defense Force base where he worked. Afterward, in Albany, he found a spiritual home at a Conservative congregation. As a single man, and given the central role of families in Judaism, Abbey was given special attention— lots of invitations to family dinners. Soon he was in a relationship deeply colored by Jewish practice.

"What locked it in was meeting my future wife, Sheryl, there. We encouraged each other; we went out to the Israeli folk-singing night at the synagogue. The following week, on Friday night, we made dinner and observed the basic practices of Jewish Friday night. We lit the candles, made the blessings, and basically started a ritual that's become dominant in our home.

"Living in the world has made me more conscious of my Jewishness almost daily. In some ways, if you're Orthodox, you don't have to think of it. Sheryl's sister teaches at a Yeshiva, goes only to kosher restaurants, her sons are in the Yidl League—that's right, 'Yidl League'—her husband works in a kosher supermarket. They never see anybody who isn't Jewish." By contrast, Abbey feels he has to work all the harder to maintain Jewish living while working in a largely secular and even hostile world.

At the newspaper, Abbey is also confronted with Jews who no longer practice their religion. Though he holds the door open, inviting many to holidays at his home, he does not proselytize, in keeping with general Jewish practice.

"You can't bring a horse to the Torah and make him read," he comments dryly. But his religion shapes work life in other ways.

"This may limit my career possibilities but I'm not going to take a job that involves working on Saturdays, and I don't think that affects anyone else in the newsroom, thankfully." And when he eats with sources or at business group banquets, Abbey's religion is made manifest in the kosher food he orders.

His faith also shapes the work he does.

"I always saw journalism as a means of doing good, to inform people about the world they live in. Even more so in today's world, knowledge is power. It is a noble task, bringing people knowledge, in business even more than in politics. That's where people spend their lives, on their jobs. Everybody pays taxes to the government, but the shape and form those taxes take are often warped by unseen forces, primarily business and powerful interests. It runs the gamut from whether a road will go through your neighborhood because a developer wanted it that way to the less mundane like there's a store opening down the street. Most media under-cover business and don't understand it."

For instance, as most local reporters quickly learn, it is not the members of the town board or city council who call the shots as much as the business interests behind them. Good business reporting, says Abbey, "will show the wires that make Peter Pan fly."

His faith also constrains and conflicts with standard journalistic practice, which can involve the most ephemeral of news. "Much of journalism is based on rumor, innuendo and sensationalism. That's a problem I have with my work."

Increasingly, Abbey chafes against the common wisdom that journalists must remain detached from community life. Many reporters, for instance, do not join civic organizations or political parties—or even vote—in order to avoid even the appearance of partiality.

"Settling more into the community makes me want to participate in that community more. Marginality is less appealing to me. The sensationalism and twisting and warping, because of our inexact science and the cavalier attitude most of us take about the impact of what we do, bother me more. I'm facing some real contradictory impulses as far as career decisions and how I square what I do with what I believe."

He has also had to balance roles at his synagogue with his professional life.

"I'm continually fending off requests to cover things. I don't want people to think they have a special line to heaven."

At the same time, Abbey wants to serve as president of his synagogue, both for personal reasons and also to carry on the legacy of a great-grandfather and a grandfather who were deeply involved in Jewish affairs.

"But the deeper I get involved on that level, the harder it is to balance my professional detachment. This year I'm going to be vice president at the synagogue, and I will be approaching people for fund-raising I have dealt with professionally. If anyone comes back to me (for help in placing a news article), I will explain that these are separate things. If that's a fiction in my own mind that most people don't get, so be it, but I will attempt to keep that distinction in my practice."

How does he discern God's will? Abbey readily admits that may be impossible.

"What's knowable is what the sages and thinkers of Judaism have attempted to discern, but I'm not capable of knowing what's wanted from me in the larger sense. I only know what is worth doing based on the principles that I believe in. I assume that it fits into a plan, but it's a plan about which I know nothing. That's the essential question that Jews come back to and back to and back to."

Though Israel, in Scripture, suffered the consequences of misdeeds, Abbey says it is unlikely in the post-Holocaust era for people to accept such a connection, since it invariably implicates the victims.

"I have no direct mystical connection. For most Jews it's 'here are the rules, follow them.' Frankly, I pick and choose, but I do the best I can."

Abbey feels he should not cover certain kinds of news, the type that verges on or amounts to gossip and slander.

"I don't cover death, cops and crime. If I have a goal, it's to help people by providing them with information that's useful in their lives and that gives them a better ability to control their destinies. Most coverage of crime is done for other reasons: exploitation, titillation." Abbey waves his flattened hand across the air in front of him as if to sweep away all the shallow horror of tabloid—and much mainstream—news.

"I just don't have an interest in that. I don't read it, I don't follow it, I don't get excited about it. I don't think anything useful comes of it. Ninety-nine times out of a hundred, especially around here, it's a kid who kills his mother or something like that, and it's very rare you're going to extrapolate societal messages out of that."

Though he does not have an agenda for his work, Abbey keeps a single purpose in mind. "There is a hidden reality to the way the world works. I mean this in practical, economic, political terms, and it's best people know that. I want, whenever possible, to rip away the false smiles and the insincere backslapping and self-promotion that accompanies most public discourse."

As he warms to his subject, Abbey grows more vehement. "When you rip away the smiles of the corrupt congressman and see those little slits of lizard eyes and the little grin and the sharp teeth in the back of his mouth and you give people a flash of the reality that underlies all this mendacity, that's pretty valuable."

But in so doing, how does a reporter avoid trading in titillation?

"You just present the information that people would not have had the time or ability to get themselves and present it in such a way that seems credible. When the information is that good, you don't have to jazz it up with flip characterizations."

I know that Abbey practices this in his work, having worked alongside him for two years. I have also asked him to edit several of my longer stories, such as the growth of fundamentalist Christian churches in upstate New York or the failure of drug treatment programs to monitor themselves. Each time, he has carefully pared away useless characterizations in order to let the facts and reporting tell the story.

His own specialty has plenty of room for good reporting.

"Business has a tremendous effect on people's lives, and it is filled with more puffery and hype than any other arena. What the president of General Electric does has ten times, a hundred times, more of an effect on the people of Schenectady (where GE has had a massive plant for a century) than what the mayor does. I mean, the mayor is the last to know."

He gives other examples, such as "the state throwing money at businesses who don't need it because that makes the governor look good." Abbey mentions the allocation of cheap, state-produced power to various, already-profitable industries or a local toy manufacturer "who, in one week, placed seventy-plus million dollars in the private capital market and the next week took a low-interest loan, a gift from the state. Come on, folks."

What about coping with the pressures of reporting, such as balancing demands of the job against one's conscience or even common sense?

"You have to do your job. As a journalist you always get the chance to reinvent yourself the next day, to snap back from a bad day in a way that most people don't have. You also have to look at things over time, take a broader view of things. Whether it's a week's worth of work or a month's work or a year's—over time the good work stands out."

Settling into a community and joining its groups, although it causes some conflict with a journalist's desire for detachment, can produce better reporting.

"Then you know how the paper's work affects the community, and your work is part of that. People read the paper, and it really affects their lives. In fact, most journalists know the least about the effect of their writing primarily because their circles are so narrow and most of their friends are in the media."

Reactions, pro and con, from friends and neighbors are one thing. More elusive, as ever with the printed word, are actual results. Though a reporter usually can't see the impact from one particular story, Abbey remembers most fondly a series of investigative stories he wrote for a New Jersey newspaper.

"People told me they would run down to the stoop to get the paper and read the stories. Years later, several people were indicted and then convicted from issues first raised in that series." Abbey can also stroll over to a nearby Ben and Jerry's ice cream store to see a story he wrote about the company in 1980, one of the first, still up on the wall.

Of course, the paycheck is the primary reward for most people who work, even journalists—who invariably possess, under a cynical front, the romantic ideal that they can indeed make a difference. But Abbey doesn't look to change the world.

"I don't need that much anymore, frankly. I have an internal sense of the impact, even if people don't tell me specifically. I hear enough in general to know there is a reaction. That's not to say there aren't days when nobody reads what I do." He drops his voice as if to reassure some unseen and troubled colleague. "You can't worry about that; you just can't worry about that."

There is also the danger of wanting to please everyone.

"My personal psychological need is to make everybody happy and to keep everybody liking me, although I understand intellectually that's not possible. I probably have been taken advantage of over time because of that, and I am now learning to assert myself more and take a stand, though I'm uncomfortable with doing so.

"In terms of getting along with other people, I'm more aware of people and not as oblivious to the scene around me as I used to be. Still, I don't have a good handle on how I'm perceived. People at the newspaper see me as far more corporate and straitlaced than I am, which may be a sign of maturity in an industry that prides itself on arrested development."

Does Jewish law, embodied in Jewish texts, provide guidelines for living in the world?

"Oh, many, many, many. Many of which are contradictory! There are the Torah and the Biblical commands and stories. Also, we have the Mishnah and the Gemorah, which comprise the Talmud. The Gemorah is the larger collection of oral law and written responses and rabbinical discussions written over several centuries that attempted to answer practical questions of life in a heterogeneous society. Around the world, Jews have almost always lived in cultures and societies they did not control. There are laws for Jewish behavior and for practical matters down to such things as where you can place a window to give yourself light and protect a neighbor's privacy if you live in a courtyard.

"The Mishnah is the basic part of the Talmud and consists of its earliest stages developed over four centuries. It contains the early level of rabbinical rulings on civil law. It is case law with specific applications, and it is amazingly contemporary in application. It is still developing."

Basically, Abbey feels directed to follow the biblical injunction "to be a light unto the world, to carry God's law and understanding of creation to the world at large." With a friend, he is working on a book tentatively entitled, *Management Advice from the Bible*. During a brief conversation at the newspaper one day, he explained why his version of the good life involves plunging into life: "It's a basic Jewish precept—have a job, be in the world."

That mission, he said at another time, "has led many Jews into social or community service and political activism." Others enter into a deeper level of observance "designed to bring about redemption of the world through religious practice." Both paths, Abbey says, can be inspired and guided by Jewish teachings and study.

"It gets down to, literally, questions like, what do you do when your neighbor's grapevines grow over the fence? Or are there times when you shouldn't put vinyl siding on your house because it will affect property values?

"Most American Jews, save the Orthodox, have no knowledge of these teachings and live their lives completely ignorant of what a lot of people say is the most important part of Judaism, the Talmud and Mishnah, which are more important than the Torah." At this, Abbey pulls back with a self-conscious smile. "But that's a lecture for another day."

He considers the perspective—sometimes clear, sometimes not—bestowed by his spiritual development.

"As much as I would like to see the hand of God in daily activities, it can be a slippery slope doing that. When you see the hand of God in good things you have to see the hand of God in bad things, and I don't think I can discern that in my daily life. I feel better than I used to believing there is some order and meaning down the road, even if I'm not capable of perceiving it. For a long time I didn't believe that at all, and over time that tends to corrode your entire outlook. I feel better about that now."

# EIGHT

Patrice Gaines

Author, inspirational writer,
Washington Post reporter

Some spiritual awakenings are more dramatic than others. Despite surviving several dangerous situations, Patrice Gaines says her transformation came "not like a turning point but more like a curve."

Three moments stand out in the life of Gaines, author of two books and a reporter at *The Washington Post*.

"Going to jail started a journey; not a dramatic journey," she says. "Later, being brutally beaten and raped made me realize I didn't want to die; I didn't have a death wish."

Moments after that assault, Gaines declined the ultimate revenge on the man who had whipped her bloody but was now asleep. She describes the scene in her memoir, *Laughing In The Dark*.

"I was standing, looking down at him, and a thought came to me, *Go get a butcher knife and stab him in the throat*. I walked into the kitchen, chose the biggest knife, one with a long, jagged edge, and walked back into the living room. He was still asleep. I stood over him, lifted the knife, and held it in the air so that the point was right over his throat.

"Time must have ceased, because while I held the knife suspended in the air I remembered my daughter sleeping in the bedroom in back. If I killed him, the police would come with their white faces and blaring red lights and they'd take me away....What would happen to her?"

The thought stayed the hand with the long knife. Gaines' life proceeded, though it was several years before she shook off the shackles of her late teens and early adulthood. By the time she was twenty-five years old, Gaines had experienced a wide range of crime, violence and self-destructiveness.

"I shot heroin, got busted for possession with the intention to distribute, and went to jail one summer in Charlotte, North Carolina. Even after that, I continued with bad choices of friends and bad choices of men, mostly abusive. I was raped twice, once viciously, and beaten. I struggled as a single mother, experienced extreme poverty, and had to beg social services for money. Almost anything I write about today, I've experienced." Gaines' composure and her calm, mellifluous voice contrasts with her recollections and bespeak the powerful foundation in spirituality laid by her parents, firmed up by her love for her mother and daughter, and topped off by her discovery that one kind of love preceded all others. In her book, she writes of her thoughts as she accepted an award for Best Commentary from the National Association of Black Journalists :

"Now you see? This is why you shot dope. This is why you went to jail. This is why you were lost. So that you could one day go out and spread the word that there is no greater love than love of self."

Even during her dark years and moments, her vocation was clear. "All I ever wanted to do was write," she says simply. While a teen, she began putting words on paper, finding a release and creativity that was otherwise inaccessible.

"At nineteen, I started a journal, which I would write in when I was feeling bad or troubled. It was easy because I didn't have the guts or the words to speak out loud about what was bothering me. I couldn't say it, but I could write it. And I felt better when I wrote about being in the middle of a life but not understanding life, about having this child or being in a relationship where I felt mistreated."

Gaines returned to the journal while in prison, and later wrote fiction. "When I came to journalism, I already loved to write," she says.

As happens with many reporters, Gaines has been frustrated by the dailiness of news writing, by the limits to exploration and creativity. She has also had to overcome the preconceived notions of editors who tend to pigeonhole reporters as, say, a deadline reporter, a good investigator, or someone who can write soft features.

"There came a point when I wanted to write longer stories, to be more creative. I wanted to write for the features section or for the magazine (*The Washington Post Sunday Magazine*). I applied and never got it, which was frustrating. I realized the editors weren't against me personally, but there is this attitude at the *Post* that if you're a Metro reporter, you can't write. I decided my options didn't lie only there; the world was wide open. I knew my true love was writing, and I always wanted to write a book. I needed to go back to that."

Her memoir came later, as an outgrowth of a personal essay she wrote for the *Post*, revealing her past life. That involved considerable risk but, as Gaines details in her book, the story virtually forced its way out of her. A fellow reporter opened the door for her. Nathan McCall, who later wrote *Makes Me Wanna Holler*, first wrote an essay for the paper about his former life of crime, a life similar to the one Gaines had led: birth and childhood in stable families with working parents, a descent into rage and violence, followed by a kind of redemption.

But before her memoir, Gaines concentrated on fiction, taking creative writing courses, studying under Gloria Naylor, and spending time at two artist colonies, Yaddo in Saratoga Springs, New York, and MacDowell in Peterborough, New Hampshire.

"Those kinds of things made me feel better," Gaines relates. "The lesson for me was that sometimes we have too narrow a definition of what success in our career is. You have to create your own options. You can't be defeated by what someone says about you."

Gaines' start in journalism came after narrowly escaping her previous life. She was caught shoplifting and spent the night in jail. The store did not pursue criminal action and her probation officer never heard about the incarceration. Gaines was scared off hard drugs. Later, she quit what had seemed a solid job after her affair with one of the owners was revealed. In these events, Gaines detected divine intervention.

"I was given another chance, a reprieve to straighten out my life," she wrote. Even the terminated affair served some purpose: "Nevertheless, my dishonorable relationship...helped me end up in a job that would change me for the better."

A position as a secretary at the *Charlotte Observer* led to some writing for the company newsletter and some research work.

"For me, it was nothing short of magic to string together words in a way that made people notice and care," Gaines says. "This was the answer to my prayers, to be able to touch people in a way that I had not been able to with my actions or the words from my mouth."

It was here Gaines received one of those painful pieces of advice that can either crush or inspire a young writer. The editor found mistakes—wordiness, slang and poor structure—in her first story, one about pets. He added a note: "An ego is too big to fit into a typewriter." The comment helped her overcome her embarrassment and concentrate on her work.

The time in Charlotte led to a summer program for minority journalists at the University of California at Berkeley and then to her first job as a reporter at the *Miami News*. She later worked for the *Washington Star*, which folded seven months after she arrived. In 1985, Gaines was hired by *The Washington Post*. She survived one crisis, when she was almost fired after managers discovered her felony conviction, which Gaines had deliberately omitted when applying. The paper's famous editor, Benjamin Bradlee, told Gaines it was her writing talent that helped her survive the ruptured trust.

Aside from her experiences, Gaines also benefited from being a bit older than many other cub reporters.

"I didn't become a reporter until I was twenty-nine, which I found out later was old," she says. "I never knew, growing up, what I wanted to be." During tough times, she would say, her deep faith and developing spirituality kept her afloat.

"There was only a short time when I wasn't sure there was a God, when I was in my early twenties. Other than that, I always believed there was more to life than what I perceived, even before my family taught me about God. I always found it a depressing thought that what you see and the way people treat each other is the only thing in life. As I got older, however, my definition of God changed, and maybe it will some more.

"My beliefs didn't become what my parents or family believed in. My mother introduced me to church, though I didn't always believe what I heard there." Her family hosted prayer meetings at home, and the Gaines children were sent to a Baptist church in the neighborhood with their grandparents.

"Since my mid-twenties, I have been reading about other religions and trying to grapple with the meaning of life." More recently, she attended a Baptist church that she liked for its Afro-centric flavor. But after several years, Gaines was discouraged by several homophobic comments from the preacher and unhelpful preaching that focused on world issues. "I was looking for something that would help me day to day," Gaines explains.

When preparing to marry her current husband, a Catholic, Gaines went through the nine-month course for potential converts, the Rite of Christian Initiation for Adults.

"I decided not to convert, but I enjoyed studying the religion." In a typically American expression of individual spirituality, Gaines says she objected to the idea that she would have to wait until she was baptized for the nuptials.

"God knew I was ready and did not have to get ready. Even if I do convert one day, I'll take from it what I can." With any religion, she says, "I don't find I always believe everything, so I take what I need and leave the rest."

More recently, Gaines has been attending a spiritualist church, aptly named Church of Two Worlds. Spiritualism originated in its contemporary form in upstate New York in the years after 1848. The two hundred thousand or more adherents in the United States believe the living can communicate with those who have "passed on." Despite the religion's exotic reputation, it stresses such practical doctrines as meditation, healthy living, and the connectedness of all life.

"For a long time, I have believed you should develop the God within you by developing all the powers and abilities God gave you. The emphasis is on study and meditation. They have meditations in church to help you become more in tune with the part of you that talks to God, to your guide and angels."

Gaines appears to have been predisposed toward believing in the action of spirits. In her memoir, she writes of a spirit sent by God being involved in the birth of her daughter. She also tells of a dream in which her recently deceased father finally expresses his pride in her—releasing her from resentment and a lifetime of hurt. Gaines was always searching, sometimes with comical desperation. At one point, Gaines and a friend read the works of Carlos Castaneda and devoured texts on positive thinking. They visited a psychic, who left Gaines frustrated. She writes, "I was more interested in asking the woman questions like: 'What is time?' and 'What is death?' than in knowing what was going to happen to me tomorrow or next year."

Today, though her searching continues, Gaines feels she has found a home for her faith.

"I never believed we die and that's it. I believed for years in reincarnation, in things my mother didn't believe. That should be the quest of each person, to define God in his or her life and develop a personal relationship with God. You should investigate, do some real research, read and study until something feels true to you, so God isn't just sitting out there, so you really feel God is here."

Her thirst for faith combined painfully with the need for it. "Because I had a troubled life in my early twenties, especially with drugs, where everything seemed dark and gloomy, I knew I had to find some way out, to really understand life, but I had a little glimmer of hope. I started meeting pop psychologists, reading a little of the Koran, investigating different religions. I was trying to find something I felt okay with. As I began to do that, I started feeling better, so my reading continued."

The exploration continued, in fits and starts, for more than a decade. Even after her self-destructive years were behind her, Gaines passed through a narrow vale, due both to the aging of her parents and grandparents and the loss of many friends to AIDS-related illnesses. She wrote of a year she spent traveling and studying:

"No matter where I was, death reached me. In thirteen months, six people in my life died, most of them people who had touched me daily, or who had profoundly affected me....Death made me judge less and love more. Death taught me that you have a say in the way you go, that you establish patterns and habits early in your life that probably determine when and, to some degree, how you die. Not obvious patterns like the kinds of people we have sex with or how much alcohol we drink, but patterns based on how much faith, love and fear we have."

As a person who asks questions for a living, Gaines is convinced she is there to learn. "When I became a journalist, I realized the people I wrote about came into my life to teach me." She calls that belief, by itself, superficial, but it led to a deeper realization in her work.

"Now I almost feel as if I come into their lives for a mutual reason, that there is a reason we're there together."

This conviction, and her dedication to the spiritual life, help Gaines take seriously the beliefs of others in her reporting and writing, leading to the sort of in-depth news features for which she is well known.

There is a growing recognition in some circles that reporters have to approach the beliefs of their subjects and readers to capture "the truth beyond the facts." In a talk to the American Society of Newspaper Editors, Shirley MacLaine traded on her reputation as a New Age guru to challenge journalists in this direction:

"The Founding Fathers of this nation understood that man's nature is essentially spiritual, and in understanding that they provided for the sanctification of human liberty. Why is the discussion of spirituality considered so publicly embarrassing, so sentimental, and, God forbid, so New Age?" MacLaine then challenged journalists to "grant an unembarrassed recognition of the spiritual dimension in the life of each individual and the role that dimension plays in the affairs of mankind."

Gaines leads in that sort of personal reporting. "I don't take my role lightly. Even if it seems like a silly story, I have been given the responsibility and opportunity to come into people's lives, and I should leave them better." She chuckles softly and adds, "Even though the media doesn't have that reputation.

"I am being given an awesome responsibility, going into people's lives and asking them personal questions and showing who they really are to the world. It just humbles me."

In her book, *Laughing In The Dark*, Gaines elaborated on her front-row seat in the theater of life:

"I saw human beings at their most fragile moments, and to my surprise, there was a beautiful by-product: At that moment when people are reacting from what seems like sheer emotions, they are most honest. There is no time to think of deceptions, no will to even try. When I questioned a mother whose daughter had been murdered in a park not far from their home, a couple whose son had hanged himself in the front yard, they did not have time or forethought to edit what they said....What came out of their mouths were the most beautiful, simple truths about life and love and death. I felt terribly fortunate to hear them."

With opportunity came responsibility and, as anyone who has received a friend's confidence knows, the deeper the truth or confession, the more one stands in awe of the person's trust in the listener. At this critical juncture, a news reporter reveling over the great insight he or she has received, may be tempted toward abuse by the idea of a "good story," one that would please the editors and be prominently displayed in the paper or magazine. Here, conscience and professional ethics temper ambition. "I try to remember that the goal isn't just to get on the front page," says Gaines.

At first, Gaines saw journalism as "an extension of life and an opportunity to learn more about life." Later, with time and experience, she grew to accept a broader role beyond personal enrichment.

"I now have the nerve or urge to believe that I can teach other people through my choice of stories. When I write about crime, I do it in a different way, not necessarily by writing about the victim but about the families of the accused." The goal, she says, is to stretch the boundaries of traditional reporting, "to get people to be more compassionate and considerate."

Swimming in such depths, Gaines, her subjects, and her readers often encounter the basic beliefs shaping and steering lives.

"There was a time recently when I had three stories in a row where I mentioned God in the lead sentence. The religion reporter and I laughed. One was about a woman who had a drug problem. She had five kids and she neglected them, stayed out all night. But every Sunday she sent them to church so they would be kept straight. One day she followed. She went straight, enrolled in college, and turned her life around.

"In another story, I wanted to find a kid, a young black guy who stayed out of trouble, since we're always writing about them when they're in trouble. I found this one guy who wanted to be a firefighter. His father had AIDS and drug problems, went through a rehabilitation program, but was sick. So now, after all these years, the son was taking care of his father. The son was the kind of guy who didn't get counted in the statistics. He was a church member as a boy and later he joined the choir. His church was the one thing that kept him straight while growing up in this chaotic family—his father was in and out of jail, his mother had him when she was sixteen. The family was not traditional, and his church helped keep him straight."

In yet another story, Gaines wrote about a different side of life in the Washington metropolitan area, where much of the city and surrounding suburbs are, by and large, segregated:

"There was a bunch of women in a Catholic church in an all-white suburb who started a support group in a housing project in Washington. What caused these women to do this was their belief that you have to act on your faith and that in so doing you make your own life better. Then the inner-city women in the support group started improving their own lives. A number of them got their high school equivalency diploma, some finished rehabilitation programs; they did things the welfare system couldn't persuade them to do before. It was the human touch that made the difference."

Her forays into this sort of reporting inspired Gaines to spread the good news. "I had considered going around talking about spiritualism in journalism, how going to work could be the same for reporters as going to church. We are faced with profound issues in our society. One day in the winter, when it was especially cold, there were these homeless people who had congregated in the lobby of *The Post,* and I had to interview them." The assignment, so close to her professional sanctum, prompted some soul-searching tempered by Gaines' own experience with self-destructive choices.

"I had to ask myself, 'What is society's responsibility to the homeless?' I knew, from my personal experience, that the situations some were in were due to choices they had made. And that's like going to church: you have to ask yourself, 'Do you write the story? Do you question yourself?' That is what I call the gift of it, of being a journalist."

Naturally, putting one's values and person on the line can be tiring. Many people manage to get through the day thanks to basic assumptions about their self-worth, their conclusions, decisions, routines. Gaines has learned to handle the self-examination.

"I now know better what I can and can't do. I used to wonder, and I still do, 'Why can't I write a story that will make everything better?' But now, I do what I can do. I can get angry or frustrated with all of us, but I am maturing. It was because of the time I spent pondering that I came to those conclusions about what I can and can't do.

"When I first entered journalism, I remember hearing that good stories deal with the basics: shelter, food, work. As my sense of religion evolved, all my stories began to boil down to a more universal theme: people's search for love and for God. Now, when I am interviewing people, I look for those things."

It is not always easy. Most subjects of news stories do not automatically volunteer their motives, never mind the basic beliefs underlying their actions and objectives. How can a writer broach the subject, under the pressure of a deadline or with people in crisis? How do you ask a person who just lost a job or spouse or reputation about his or her soul?

Sometimes you don't have to ask—religious belief may

simply emerge as the center of a situation or a person's life or a news item.

"I was interviewing a guy who was serving thirty-five years to life for a crime he said he didn't commit," Gaines says. "He was such a peaceful guy, so I asked him how he could live with it, and he really opened up to me about his faith. Earlier, I would not have been able to approach the topic; it seemed that God was unapproachable unless you were a religion writer. Now I question these things, because so often people, for instance, join a neighborhood patrol group because they feel they should. There are so many times you can reduce a story down to very basic things, such as the need for faith and love. All I have to do is get near the subject, and they enjoy talking about it."

Without mentioning faith or belief, many veteran reporters and editors advise younger colleagues to dig deep. But often they mean to follow the money trail or to seek out the secret documents, the hidden court records, the land deeds proving a questionable real-estate transaction. Such advice is the basis of much good work. But why stop there? As Shirley MacLaine observed to the newspaper editors, "Newspapers have won Pulitzer Prizes identifying hidden sources of corruption in government, hidden sources of pollution, hidden motives that have subverted commerce or adversely affected the economy." So why not do more "in-depth reporting of the spiritual character of the participants and the religious nature of events...?"

Gaines believes that these lines of inquiry produce full-bodied journalism.

"It makes for much better stories, because it is the truth—just to get to the core of people's actions and lives. Some reporters stop before they get to the core, and the reader may surmise that this is a God-filled person they are reading about, but they shouldn't have to surmise a person's beliefs any more than they have to with other facts in a story, such as where or when something happened."

To maintain her own spiritual life, Gaines meditates most mornings, usually for thirty minutes, and takes steps to keep a focus on the transcendent and enduring in life.

"It helps, even when I don't sit down to meditate, to have a time to myself. I like quiet periods when I am at home, in the evenings. I always try to read something before bed that feeds my soul. It may be a book about healing. Last night I was reading about someone who had a near-death experience. I pray all the time, in the car, wherever.

"I always pray before I interview someone, on the way to the interview, or when I'm setting it up. I generally pray that we'll find this common ground, particularly if I am concerned that the person will not talk to me, or when they seem irritated with me or are just not open. I pray that God will help me find a greater truth, and that I will use the story to glorify God."

The spiritual has become so uppermost in her life that Gaines has written a new book entitled *Moments Of Grace*.

"It's a spiritual book about changing your life," she says. "I get so many people asking me how I changed my life. It's a step-by-step process. The book doesn't say there is one way to do it, but there are some things you can't get around."

Despite her time shooting heroin, Gaines does not believe she was an addict, nor did she recover from the use of drugs through one of the popular and effective twelve-step or self-help programs.

"On my book tour, these people said to me, 'You know everyone's an addict. All addicts are in denial.' I'd say maybe I was a recreational user. But there was a time when I just was always high, a period when I knew I had a problem."

Today, Gaines has her own program for keeping on the spiritual beam. "I do enough things daily and weekly that keep me on track: the books I read, the people I see. I do things to build my spiritual muscles. All my friends aren't journalists. What helps particularly is talking to people out in the community. Meditating and praying allow me to maintain my balance. If a challenge comes up, something usually reminds me of God or my spirituality and I don't find it hard to face the challenge.

Just as with physical exercise, dropping a program of spiritual exercise can hurt, despite all the previous effort.

"Even people who work to maintain the spiritual life get to the point where they say, 'I'm cured' and they don't maintain it," warns Gaines.

At work, Gaines keeps out of office politics and competition.

"I try not to be affected by what goes on in the newsroom, who's on page one. I've always had the attitude that I would succeed no matter what." The competitiveness of newspapers and most reporters leaves her unperturbed. Faith helps; so does having published a well-received book, she admits. Editors now regard her more seriously and defer to her suggestions more often.

"That was the funny thing about discovering I can compete in this world. The book and publicity helped me gain a little prestige on the job. Now, I get to write and choose the stories I want, and I have a little more control."

Being focused on the reporting and writing, rather than on climbing up the hierarchy at *The Washington Post*, helps Gaines avoid some ambitions and disappointments.

"To different degrees, there were times when I wasn't as happy there as others. What helped me was that I never wanted to be an editor or in management."

There are still times when her ethics and beliefs conflict with those in authority over her. Once Gaines was working on a profile of several convicts. She refused to identify in print where one was being held, because to do so would have put the man's life in danger.

"One of my editors dismissed that, saying that the convict was a murderer and didn't deserve special treatment," Gaines explains. "I thought, 'What is my responsibility as a human being, as a person of God?' I happen to work as a reporter, but I have to live as myself. In the end, I went to my editor's supervisor. I argued the case and he agreed. I always have to ask myself, 'Will I be able to live with myself after this story runs?'

"I don't always come up on the right side of things. I wrote a story four or five years ago about a woman who died in a fire, and I mentioned that she was an alcoholic. I was troubled afterward. In the story, I talked about the bad things in her life; I didn't talk about the fact that she was a mother who had tried to raise her children. What did anyone gain by that story destroying someone after their death? In that case, one of her relatives called me crying. I didn't say that much. I'd worked on the story with another reporter and had gotten caught up in the competitiveness. I forgot what was really important. I wanted a front-page story."

Today, Gaines keeps it simple: "I try now not to think about where a story goes; I just try to use each one to teach the principles I believe in."

NINE

Antoinette Bosco

Syndicated columnist, newspaper editor, book author

Right from the start, Antoinette Bosco will tell you, "I'm not a great Catholic." But in her fourteen years as executive editor of a prizewinning weekly newspaper, syndicated columnist, and author of six books, Bosco has always recognized a direct connection between a writer's moral beliefs and her words on the page, regardless of topic.

"Only about fifteen or twenty percent of my writing is on spiritual subjects," says Bosco. "But in every story I do, in every question I ask, in every approach, I'm working from the values I live by, which is a real commitment to honesty and fairness and justice. That's how you work it out in all that you do. It's not by standing there saying, 'I'm very spiritual,' because to be truly spiritual, it has to be ingrained, it has to be second nature."

Writers often feel that they operate in a vacuum. Readers rarely notice bylines and even less often do they contact a journalist to report their reactions to a story. So when a woman who read Bosco's book on being a single parent wrote to say the volume "saved my life," it meant a lot. "She had seven kids and her husband left her," explains Bosco. After meeting for lunch several times, the two became friends.

Bosco remembers a time when she was registering for graduate courses. "There was this beautiful woman standing there and she had four lovely kids with her." When the two introduced themselves, the woman said, "Antoinette Bosco! You see those kids? It's all your fault I have those kids." As it turned out, the woman had read a story Bosco wrote about a children's home and the shortage of foster care parents.

"She was so touched that she contacted the home, and these were the four foster kids she had gotten," Bosco relates. "You could see she loved those kids. This is how it comes back to you. I didn't write that story with the idea that I was going to change the world, but maybe the little corner I touched did change for those four kids."

The real question for those who know her is whether Toni Bosco ever closes her eyes and goes to sleep. A single parent for many years, she raised seven children, including one she adopted after spotting him cold and hungry in a post office.

At the time of our first conversation, Bosco was executive editor of *The Litchfield County Times* in northwest Connecticut, a prizewinning, well-regarded weekly. Her readers ranged from dairy farmers to Manhattan millionaires with vacation homes in the area to famous writers, dancers and artists who treasure the wooded hills of Litchfield.

Bosco is a compact woman of medium height with wavy brown hair. Her dress and coiffure suggest a care—but not a preoccupation—with appearance. From close up, she gives the impression of a well-oiled engine in high gear, emiting power and energy without noise or smoke. She writes a syndicated column for *Catholic News Service* and pens op-ed pieces for other Connecticut newspapers. She meets monthly with a prayer group, regularly visits the nearby Benedictine Abbey of Regina Laudis—a center for spiritual travelers—and reads about six books a week. On top of that, she has a wide variety of friends. When one is in need, Bosco is likely to swoop down with a plate of lasagna or cold cuts and an afternoon of listening or talking.

All this energy and love springs from her faith. Though Bosco is quick to point out her occasional disagreements with the Catholic hierarchy, the Church has influenced her life in different and profound ways at several crucial points.

Bosco entered the College of Saint Rose in Albany, New York, when she was seventeen. "I was also entering the torment of the damned, asking, what's it all about? Is life real? I was reading everything, and I had a religion professor, very fatherly, who said 'You're hitting your head against a brick wall, and all you'll get is a bloody head.' He said 'Just accept, just accept.'"

And so Bosco did. She became a "real rah-rah Catholic and a defender of the faith," she says. At thirty-seven, when her marriage broke up, however, her old faith was out of date.

"I was left to support six of my seven kids—and then I started asking very different questions. That was the real turning point. I had to face what my life was really all about and what my faith meant."

"It was," she adds, "not the last time, since I had later to suffer the loss of my two sons. That's what my book, *Finding Peace Through Pain: The True Story Of A Journey Into Joy,* is about. God comes closer, blow by blow, but sometimes, just before he comes closer, he's really kind of far away."

Armed with this evolved faith, Bosco explains, the death of her youngest son, Peter, "never shook my faith, which is interesting since it was a suicide." Neither was her faith rocked years later by the murders of her son John and his wife, Nancy.

Bosco develops her beliefs via prayer ("all the time, in my car, when I get up, mostly prayers of thanksgiving") and study. She reads a great deal. "I'm a bookaholic. I pick up a book and I get really excited about what I'm going to learn," says Bosco. "I've gotten to be almost sixty-five, and this passion for reading has increased, not decreased."

True, not everyone could do that much homework, Bosco admits. "I read very fast; I get by on six hours of sleep; I don't watch much television; and I don't spend much time on the phone," she says. Although it may seem a demanding schedule, keeping one's priorities in line sweeps aside many distractions.

"I've learned in life that we always have time to do what we really want to do. Usually when we say we don't have the time, we're mostly saying we don't have time to do things we're not that interested in doing. If we really want to do something, we do have the time."

What sort of practical code does Bosco use in her daily march to meet deadlines and, until recently, manage reporters, get out the paper, and still remain true to her beliefs?

"Just be a loving person in all your relationships. You have to reach out as a loving person." That may have been hard in a newsroom, but Bosco worked at it. For instance, if she overheard the receptionist rudely turning away an unwanted visitor, "I'd go out there and not let that happen. There is a real air of civility that we have to have. A sense that every person is important is a part of me, since I believe in the oneness of all creation."

Bosco still tries to follow the advice of her father, an Italian immigrant who ran a meat market in Albany, New York. He told her that, in addition to being *istruito*, or well-instructed, she should be *educato*, wise and compassionate. Today Bosco would give the same advice to a young reporter: Have a solid foundation in values and beliefs, be true to them, and do not fear having those beliefs shaken or your ego bruised.

"One of the challenges of life is to be courageous," she explains. "And courage sometimes means being willing to acknowledge one's weakness."

Of course, in a business with big egos, keeping one's own in line can be hard. "I really have to work on the pride issue," says Bosco. "Doesn't everybody?" In an argument with her boss, Bosco once denied having a big ego but offered that she had a strong one.

In journalism, praise is scant and professional help from superiors is rare. Reporters need to be their own best critic and fan at the same time. Years back, a bullying editor at a small paper in upstate New York used to tell his young reporters, "It's not a slap-on-the-back profession."

So is a strong ego necessary?

"I like people who are spiritually evolved, because they are in charge of their egos," Bosco maintains. "When they get into a position of power, they're not going to abuse that power." Power, if ego-driven, can hurt the people in the news and warp those who write the news.

"I have seen too many reporters cut down to size when they didn't deserve it. I wonder how many people left journalism because they couldn't take the ego-bashing." She blames the problem on insecure superiors with "unevolved souls." Perhaps the only good that comes from this sort of hothouse of conceit and fear is that it inspires writers to grow all the more in their own spirituality.

Bosco's personal faith is often the key she turns to get inside her subjects and readers. Better journalism results. "I don't see any contradiction between religion and spirituality and the things we call news or objective science or facts. Everything in life is absolutely bound up with what we are here for, and that's when we get into religion and spirituality.

"In a story I did recently, the people are rich. They have a place here and one in Montana. While talking to them, I realized they discovered something in Montana—they discovered beauty. At first, it sounded like a surface story, but I started asking, 'What was it that struck a chord in you?' They said, 'There was just something about the earth.' They may not realize they are entering their spiritual dimension until you get them going deeper inside."

Intuition, preparation and good questions are crucial for a good reporter. "You just get a one-two-three resume out of people if you don't ask the right questions," Bosco insists. "I always ask the questions that lead me in the direction of 'what makes this person tick?'"

Researching persons—especially celebrities—helps; so does a personal touch. While interviewing a wealthy man who had endowed a twenty-five thousand dollar fiction prize, Bosco hit a wall.

"I couldn't get anywhere with this man." Then she remembered that he had retired early, so Bosco mentioned her own pending retirement. "'I'm thinking of it and I'm scared,' I said. 'Were you scared?' He was so taken off guard by that question that he started to answer it, and suddenly all his protective crusts were gone.

"The next thing you know you're touching that spiritual core, and you find out there's something else this person has or needs or wants or is searching for. After spending three hours with the man, I had to leave. He wanted to introduce me to his new young wife and bring me through the house. Why? There was something he was learning from me.

"I always hope that every person I meet feels a little bit better about himself or herself, about life, about the earth. As a writer and as a journalist, I feel that's part of what I should give. I shouldn't just take.

"Sometimes I'll ask people I can't seem to break down, 'Are you more like your mother or your father?'" That question, she says, is great for "stopping people in their tracks and getting them thinking in a different direction."

Bosco also accepts that some people may not deserve to be interviewed. "I have met people I truly think are in the absolute womb in terms of any development of themselves. They don't seem to know or care or be aware of the fact that being alive means having something to do with how we relate to one another. We're not talking the same language. It's like the tower of Babel. So I avoid certain people and won't bother doing an interview with them. The first sin of journalism is to bore people; and I want my work to be entertaining, to be lively, to be informative; and I want it to be inspiring."

These approaches are easier in profile stories, which treat the personal as a matter of course. But what about the daily news stories, the fires and murders, the town board or city council meetings, elections and municipal budgets that are the stuff of life for most reporters and involve routine interviews with public officials?

"I'll say something like 'What about accountability?' Or I'll ask, 'Do you operate on a set of values? And if so, what are they?'"

Judging how well subjects live up to their professed values is another matter, one Bosco hesitates to undertake. "No one can get inside another person," she says. For example, Bosco recognizes that some political candidates will do anything short of "morally prostituting" themselves to get into office.

"Now, if they have a good motivation for getting into office, maybe that's okay. But then they get into office and they find out they're not in full control and they're not free agents and they have to compromise and give in." What looks like lying may just be part of holding elected office, she says charitably. The ideal and the real will always conflict, and Bosco says reporters should wade right in.

"The question is, 'How do we reconcile our beliefs and our desires to make the world better with the everyday realities we have to deal with?'" Nothing comes easy, according to Bosco. Religion was never meant to make us comfortable. Jesus' message was a message of disruption. To be Christian means to be uncomfortable.

"We could walk away and seek comfort—but then we'd

never be challenged. And if we're not challenged, do we ever grow? And doesn't spirituality mean we're supposed to be growing?"

Yet, even if a journalist develops her faith and accepts the spiritual side of the people she writes about and for, she needs a daily code of beliefs to carry with her.

"If you're a spiritual person, it comes out in subtle ways and in everything you do. If you've got a solid, firm base of honesty, justice and spirituality—no matter how it came to you—it will come through in how you treat others and do the work you do."

Bosco refers to the catch-all rule she had for her children: "'Never do anything to deliberately hurt anyone else or yourselves.' They said I was sneaky since that covered everything. But even for a reporter covering town meetings, if you're never going to deliberately hurt anyone, that means you're going to have to be careful about honesty, about justice, about getting things right."

Bosco also remembers how fragile a thing faith is, "how tomorrow it may be all dark and black. The most important thing for me is to remember how fragile we are, how fragile our beliefs can be, and that we have to constantly keep our humility. I have to say, 'Wherever I stand, I am in the inner circle of God's arms.' I have to hold on to that belief when I'm cold and it's dark. That's what really keeps me going."

With the code in hand, how does a reporter deploy it? Can she follow an agenda? Yes, says Bosco. "I started out with an agenda," she explains. Bosco recalls the electrifying talk she heard as a college freshman from a priest who declared, "You can change the world." So when she needed to earn extra money as a young mother, Bosco began writing freelance articles for the Catholic press. Here a desire to change the world cooperated with a strong ego. Later, Bosco wrote for *The Long Island Catholic*, a diocesan newspaper.

"I still think you have to change the world," she says.

"What you report and how you report has to have the motivation of exposing what's wrong and exposing what's good in order to make the world better. And if we don't do that as journalists, what are we in there for?

"In newswriting, everything is a judgment call. Everything from the stories you go after to how you go after them."

She gives an example of a seminar for newspaper editors hosted by Connecticut's Senator Christopher Dodd in Washington, D.C.

"The question was, 'Well, I'm covering the seminar, what then do I write about?' That's where what you consider important comes in. I chose to focus on what's happening economically in this country, in a recession and a recovery, and what's happening on the job scene and why it is happening. Then I could go into what's happening to people's lives. It is a moral problem, this matter of what you choose to cover."

Litchfield County, one of the richest counties in a well-to-do state, posed special challenges to an editor who takes seriously the teachings of Jesus. "The wealth of the area gave me a problem," says Bosco. So she worked to represent the entire region in the paper. Unlike many larger papers that ignore farmers until they are bankrupt or under water, *The Litchfield County Times* has a regular agricultural page. Bosco has written or assigned many articles on the shortage of affordable housing, on the homeless and hungry, on food banks and soup kitchens. "I know poverty," Bosco notes. "I grew up in poverty, and I knew it as a single mother raising six children."

Sometimes bearing witness can be uncomfortable. At one of the few private dinners she has attended, Bosco heard her table companions pooh-pooh the need for "cheaper homes" in the area, referring to houses with price tags of $250,000. "I finally opened my mouth and said, 'Excuse me, but a quarter-million-dollar house is not an affordable one.' And I just took off about what it means when you're trying to raise a family and you can't raise the money to buy a home and what is an affordable house." At the end, there was silence until one of the other guests thanked Bosco for opening their eyes.

Many journalists, eager to do good and expose evil, might lament that they don't have the opportunity Bosco does as an author and columnist. Though sympathetic, she replies that luck is a matter of being prepared and focused on your goals. In a television documentary about accomplished men and women, Bosco was struck by one similarity:

"The bottom line in each was that they knew what they wanted to do, they were determined to do it, and they let nothing stand in their way."

In the process of daily work as a writer and editor, can one remain charitable and loving? With all her drive and determination, Bosco admits, "I overwhelm people. I work at triple-speed." Perhaps fittingly for a forward-motion person, she betrays a certain blind spot in her self-awareness.

"I don't really know how other people in a working relationship relate to me," she says. But her beliefs are obvious, to a point. "They may not know I believe in Jesus, but they do know I operate on more than just this level." To make her case sensitively, Bosco may sometimes quote Confucius rather than Jesus.

Despite all her ideals, Bosco emphasizes: "I don't walk around with one foot in heaven. If we learn anything at all, we learn it in this world. This is where we are. We put the coffee on. We do the dishes. We take care of the runny noses with the kids."

In difficult circumstances, as when she has had to fire people, honesty and acceptance have been the best policy, Bosco says. "If something has to be, it has to be, and you can't worry about your ego or if someone is going to like you. The bottom line is being fair and just in all your relationships." The goal of spiritual development, she says, "should be to become a blessed presence to others."

The financial difficulties of earning a living in journalism are well-known to Bosco. She first entered the business to pick up extra money as a young mother, then later continued freelancing in addition to her regular jobs as editor and writer for *The Long Island Catholic*, as an assistant professor at the State University of New York at Stony Brook, and as editor of *The Litchfield County Times*. In earlier years, she gave talks on such issues as single parenting, the topic of her fifth book.

Raising her children alone and working endless hours sent Bosco near her limits. "There were times I wanted to throw in the towel. I was a feeding station. I had to give and give and give. The truth of the matter is that I just loved my kids. Would I want to do it over again? No, I would not. Would I? Yes."

Her assessment is as fundamental an expression of faith and its fruits as one will find. But here, the nature of writing, which she calls "a special vocation," helped.

"Writing is very therapeutic. You're always going out of yourself. You can't be depressed for too long."

How does all this translate into her words on the page? Aside from insisting on the highest standards in all reporting, Bosco has had her reporters write about homelessness, poverty and people who are disadvantaged. Additionally, she has written and assigned many articles on spiritual and religious topics. These subjects, overlooked by most editors, have drawn the biggest response from readers. In her own writing, she says, "I have tackled every single human rights issue you can think of."

In her opinion columns for secular newspapers, she has introduced readers to new spiritual avenues such as current findings regarding the body-mind relationship. Bosco has written about the hints at the eternal provided in near-death experiences. One piece charted how both Easter and Passover allow us to make sense of our pain. The topic is further explored in *Finding Peace Through Pain*. She has also reminded her readers that while the rich got richer during the

1980s and 1990s, the poor and disadvantaged ended up much worse off. In a freelance article for the Albany *Times Union*, she introduced readers to her father. In his old Albany meat market, he would dutifully record the debts of his poorer customers on scraps of butcher paper that would mysteriously disappear by day's end. This lesson in Christian charity—though in a secular newspaper—drew many favorable reactions.

"People remember what's human and what touches them," says Bosco. Never has there been a backlash against her implicit religiosity. Instead, articles with spiritual insight are in demand.

"Are they going to read a story all the way through about yet another artist or yet another businessman or yet another somebody else who invented some little gadget? No. They want to read a story about a local woman who went to the Abbey of Regina Laudis and knocked on the door and said, 'I haven't been good to God.'

"Everybody wants their soul touched, and the only way to touch a soul is by telling a story of a soul that's been touched. That's the only way."

In her syndicated columns for *Catholic News Service*, Bosco can write more directly on religious matters. In these, she can preach on the value of silence, on the proven relation between prayer and healing, and on the miracle of sunshine, both actually and as a symbol of the Risen Christ. In one moment, she finds transcendence in the quotidian and unexpected, and in the next she refers to the latest scientific research or to the ancient insights of the desert fathers. In a kind of two-track approach, she reaches out to believers and skeptics alike.

Though established and confident, how does Bosco keep going in a tiring and skeptical profession? What sustains her? Realism helps. "I can't change the world, but I could change the little part I touch," she says.

Bosco also likes having a good rapport with writers and

reporters she has work with. "I have done more teaching as an editor than in all the years I taught at the university. If anyone approaches me and I sense that they have something to say and can be trained, I'll put the time in and work with them." For instance, a secretary at *The Litchfield County Times* wanted to change careers but had no college degree. Bosco had her write some features and trained her bit by bit so that she later became the paper's assistant editor and then a top editor for a major publishing chain in Connecticut.

For personal support and spiritual edification, Bosco reaches out to friends in religious orders, to her spiritual director, and to her extended family.

"I go to the Abbey of Regina Laudis as often as I can. I take my quiet time for meditation and prayer in the evenings, on weekends, whenever I can, or I'll get up an hour early. I don't want to sound like a saint, because I'm not. If I didn't have so far to go, I wouldn't have to do all these things."

"I pray," Bosco says, "all the time. When I'm driving, I'm praying every time my mind is not totally focused on something else. I am conscious that I am a child of God, and I'm thanking God for life and everything else."

Thirty years ago, Bosco wrote as a young woman who needed money and was sure she had something to say. "But now, I've gone past the idea of a big ego. I've learned a lot from my work. And writing has a very strong element of teaching in it. If you do an article about a waste dump in your town, you're doing more than reporting it. You're also teaching people about what the issues are, just by the people you quote and how you arrange the story."

But opportunity must be balanced by gratitude, humility and responsibility. "I feel privileged to have had the opportunity to teach," she says. "I teach budding journalists that 'the I's' have it: Information, Inspiration, Integrity.'"

Given the nature of her work—writing for readers—the act of giving in print enriches Bosco most of all. "I feel that what we have been given and learned are to be used and passed on, and the passing on is as important as the using. If I can't pass on what I know, what good is it? It will die with me. If I have one goal now, it is to write something that will live past me."

TEN

Terry Anderson

Former Associated Press Mideast Bureau Chief

For Terry Anderson, behaving out of religious convictions makes perfect sense in journalism or, for that matter, any other field.

"In a competitive business, behaving decently is the best way to get ahead. Ideals are not what we aspire to one day before we die. Religion and Christianity offer extremely practical guidelines for living. Being selfish is not an efficient way to get ahead. What *is* a good way to get ahead is to be caring and forgiving and considerate in general, while always working hard.

"You don't have to hurt or destroy other people to be a success in any field. It's the same for nations—when we make foreign policy selfishly, it doesn't work. When it's done based on ideals, it does."

That Anderson switches easily from the personal to the global may not surprise those familiar with his story. In March 1985, when he was the chief Middle East correspondent for the Associated Press, Anderson was kidnapped in West Beirut by Shiite terrorists. Though his abductors were Islamic fundamentalists, Anderson prefers to call them terrorists and depict their use of the Koran and Islam as misguided. He was held captive for nearly seven years, much of that time chained to a wall in various hideouts. The story of his captivity, told in the book, *Den of Lions*, which he authored with his wife,

Madeleine, is also a diary of his spiritual pilgrimage to a deep faith in God.

Just six months before being grabbed off the street by armed gunmen, Anderson returned to the Catholic church of his birth and baptism. He recites a poem that also appears in his book:

> I'm not Catholic by conviction,
>
> or through belief that this one
>
> road is better than the rest.
>
> I cannot say that I've accepted
>
> all the teachings, and certainly
>
> I've failed to keep this narrow path.
>
> If I could choose, I think I'd be a Quaker,
>
> or a Buddhist, even Hindu—reincarnation's
>
> such an elegant and reassuring thought.
>
> But I can't—my parents chose before me.
>
> And though I've spent a large part
>
> of my life trying to choose otherwise,
>
> one still half hour in an
>
> empty church defies all logic.
>
> I am what both my fathers made me,
>
> and I'm content to find myself at home again.

Anderson explains his faith and its implications. Some of the latter, in political terms, is revealed in his syndicated columns.

Terry Anderson

"I remain a convinced Christian and Catholic," he says, "which I see in practical terms as a matter of trying to live as best as I can in conformance with those beliefs. Politically, I am pretty much of a liberal and a progressive, which is a natural outgrowth of my Christianity, though I know that when politics is influenced by religion it's usually more on the conservative side. I don't understand that, because if ever there was a liberal political figure, it was Jesus."

In both his opinion pieces and his political reform efforts, Anderson says, several themes predominate.

"My concern is with education, freedom of speech, social welfare. My dismay is with the way current approaches to government, both in Washington and Albany, seem focused on depriving people of social support. And that entirely opposes the way I feel as a Christian."

Advocating certain causes and explaining the religious or moral underpinnings for such positions remain different things. Anderson eschews strident religiosity in the political forum and avoids writing in his column about how his spiritual beliefs shape his public positions. "I don't specifically say it, but my political and religious feelings are very congruent attitudes."

Not that he was always devout. Anderson grew up in the town of Albion in western New York, where the landscape completes the transition from the hills and valleys of the East to the rolling flatness of the Midwest. His mother was a convert, and she brought Anderson to Sunday Mass and religious instruction. "I was raised as a Catholic, but I spent a long time as a young man, till I was about thirty-five, astray from the church. I was agnostic. I returned to the church in 1984."

One shock upon his return—as for anyone absent from the Catholic Church between the 1950s and the 1980s—was the extent to which the Church had transformed itself under the impetus of the times and, particularly, of the Second Vatican Council. Most Catholics in the United States embraced the sweeping changes of Vatican II and its call for a church of, by, and for all members, rather than the strictly hierarchical institution that existed before 1960.

"Particularly in rural areas, it was a very conservative church in the 1950s," Anderson recalls. "When I returned out of personal need, I guess, I was very surprised to find the American church one of the most liberal."

As it turned out, Anderson had little time to acquaint himself with this transformed Catholic Church. Six months after his "reconversion," he was kidnapped. But in his memoir, he writes movingly of the simple moment of truth, reached in late 1984 while sitting in a church in Sunderland, England. Drawn there, he sat in a pew, contemplated a crucifix and then, in his heart, felt as if he had returned home. Anderson writes, and still speaks, of the great relief he felt in recognizing what and who he was, of realizing he was a Catholic, no matter what he had done between his youth and that time.

Even during his agnostic period, Anderson accepted the role of religion in the lives of people and had read widely in world faiths such as Hinduism, Buddhism, Judaism and others, though largely out of intellectual curiosity. He had also reflected on the roles of the church of his childhood and of other religions in politics and history.

"I was troubled by the worldly parts of our church as so many people have been," he says. "Admittedly, I was caught up by its structure rather than its faith, and the church as a structure has not been particularly blameless. I also worked as a correspondent in some violent areas, so I made some attempt to make sense of it all."

This theme recurs throughout *Den of Lions*, as Anderson, thrown back on his own thoughts and feelings, copes with his captivity and the men behind it. Despite that experience, and the world-weariness of many in journalism, cynicism has not been a problem for Anderson. The opposite—a painfully derived but deeply cherished bedrock of belief—sustained him during the endless ordeal.

"When I speak of my experience in the Middle East, I speak of faith because it was a strong part of getting me through those years," he explains. But in newsrooms, Anderson admits, being frank about religious convictions can cause discomfort.

"An openly Christian journalist is sometimes looked at with some suspicion. Writers learn to be skeptical; it's part of our tools. Quite often, there is some suspicion that one who has strongly held beliefs is not quite trustworthy in reporting. That suspicion is without basis. There are a good many completely Christian and excellent journalists around."

Such strong beliefs, far from contradicting the aims of fairness and objectivity in journalism, actually complement the profession, Anderson believes.

"Being objective does not mean you have to refrain from showing evil as evil. Journalists are supposed to seek the truth and tell it. That, of course, is a value that was very strong on Jesus' list."

He sees some conflict, however, between the witness to reality of a Christian and the readiness of many to judge in the name of Christ.

"Seeking truth is a major requirement laid out by Jesus: truth in all things. Fanaticism puts you in conflict with your own faith. Those who are most adamant in judging others are not being quite Christian."

What about the spiritual life of the people whom journalists cover? Does their religious faith or practice matter? Should it be scrutinized, examined, discussed, reported? Anderson says he has always been fascinated by the beliefs of those he covered, even during his agnostic years.

"One reason for my fascination with Buddhism and Judaism was the absolute conviction and faith of many believers." But generally, Anderson says, he was a typical reporter when contemplating the faithful of any sect or religion.

"People of very strong religious beliefs scared me. It didn't come up very often. I was almost always a street reporter; I was out on the street and I covered events. Frequently, that involved covering radical, fundamentalist members of various sects. Shiite fundamentalists, Christian fundamentalists —I always saw them in a political, not a religious, context."

When it came time to write a religion story, Anderson was straightforward and conscientious. He mentions, almost offhandedly, reporting on the "Hidden Christians" in southern Japan, descendants of people who had converted under Iberian missionaries centuries ago and remained faithful despite persecution and isolation. The Japanese novelist Shusaku Endo has written achingly austere stories of these people and the priests who ministered to them.

"They spent two hundred fifty years in hiding, from the beginning to the end of the Tokugawa Era," Anderson describes. "I did the story as almost any other journalist would do it—reasonably, objectively.

"Religion is most often badly covered in the secular press. We tend to report surface events—the election of a pope, the conflict in a diocese—almost like we do politics." Writers and journalists, he says, could do a better job if they understood the religious motivations of the people in the news, famous or otherwise.

"People's spiritual beliefs are a strong part of their character, their motivation. And we generally leave it alone, unless they are extremely open about it. With ordinary, believing people, it isn't acknowledged as strongly as it should be." In fact, the media often ignore some obvious spiritual values of society. He gives an example. "The spirit of giving is alive and well in the United States. I just read the other day that total giving to charities rose to about one hundred thirty billion dollars. The U.S. is the biggest in terms of charitable giving in the world. Yet we are seen as selfish and self-indulgent."

Anderson notes that this reticence is not unique to journalism. When he returned home from his seven years as a captive in the Middle East, he was counseled by several psychiatrists. Only one, a devout Christian, explored with Anderson the spiritual dimensions of his experience.

"He was one of the few openly religious psychiatrists I ever met. We talked several times about how a completely secular psychiatrist or psychologist could possibly understand the motivations of a person of deep faith."

And now that Anderson is often on the other side of the reporter's notebook or microphone, he is sometimes asked about his beliefs and values, especially since these played such a strong role in his experience. Reporters, he says, "seem intrigued that I will talk about it in straightforward terms."

Is there a personal code he carries through the day's march?

"Sure. Try not to hurt people; try to do things that make me feel good. I think I'm a fairly decent human being. I have faults, some of them serious. In my actions, I try to contribute something because that makes my life worthwhile."

He works with the Vietnamese Memorial Association, which is building forty elementary schools in that country where he once served as a Marine. He serves on the board of directors of the Committee to Protect Journalists, which monitors attacks on reporters around the world. In February 1996, he began hosting a weekly radio show.

According to his account in *Den of Lions*, Anderson thought throughout his captivity of how he hoped to one day bring his life and will into harmony with his Christianity. His humble admission that he could do so only with the help of God resonates in his conversation today.

Anderson and the other captives had a prayer book written by an English evangelist who felt Jesus' teaching, "Ask and you shall receive," is meant to be taken literally. In his cell, Anderson demurred and concluded that the believer should ask only for patience and strength to endure whatever comes.

Acceptance of himself by himself offers Anderson some of his greatest solace. The lesson, learned during an experience most people will not endure, perseveres in all circumstances.

"You go through all of these things about guilt, about frustration, about anger, and what you finally come to is acceptance," he explains. "It doesn't mean hopelessness. When you say, 'I accept that I have serious faults,' it doesn't mean that you are resigned to having them forever. When you accept a situation that can't change, that doesn't mean that you stop trying to change it."

Anderson's philosophy translates into highly visible action. For one, he is now able to participate in what he once only observed. For instance, he chairs the national advisory board of the Interfaith Alliance, a group founded to present a mainstream political voice for people of faith—Christians, Jews, Moslems, Unitarians—as a counter or even in opposition to the Christian right.

"I'm highly active politically, now that I am no longer a journalist. I've always been fascinated by politics. I firmly believe it's an obligation, especially for people who want to change things and make them better. Politics is not the only way, but it is a major way. If I say, 'Gee, I feel sorry for the poor,' yet do not advocate and work for policies that I think are correct or against policies that I think are wrong, I am not carrying out in acts what I say I believe."

Whether the action is taken through writing or through politics, is Anderson ever frustrated with a lack of results?

"The world changes slowly. Yes, it is frustrating to report or do work on a bad situation and hope that will change things, and then have nothing happen. Quite often reporting changes things fairly quickly. Journalism is not going to eliminate evil from the world, but it can change a lot of situations for the better. Certainly, it is absolutely a necessary part of a free and open political system."

Anderson's reflections as a captive, plus his experience

on the other side of journalism—as a subject of stories—have widened his perspective on news professionals. Though he talks like a man ready to give anyone the benefit of the doubt, he is harsh on writers who abuse the public trust or betray their craft.

"I am contemptuous of them when they do their job badly, or when the value of their calling makes them egotistical, that is, above others. Journalists have a lot of faults. We need to understand why we're held in low esteem. People hold us in low regard not because they're stupid or perverse, but because we've done something that offends them or we have failed to make them understand why the things we do may be necessary."

Quite frequently, Anderson says, journalists don't get the basic facts right. "If you're an ordinary person, having your name in a newspaper article is the most exciting thing that's happened to you this year. If some reporter gets it wrong, that's going to be highly irritating." In the articles and broadcasts about himself, "Generally, the quality goes from good to bad to indifferent," Anderson says. "Much of it is pretty good and some is pretty bad. One newspaper did an article about me without ever calling."

Often as a reporter, he says, "We're so convinced that what we're doing is right and important that we fail to see things from the point of view of the people we're writing about. It only takes one bad journalist to mess up a lot of people's attitudes." Given his experience, Anderson is particularly outraged by certain excesses. "The ugliest part of our business is the exploitation of victims and the out-and-out *de facto* glorification of their oppressors. That isn't why we do it, we're trying to convey the truth; but it happens."

Though some abuses result from the desire to beat another newspaper or station to the story, Anderson doesn't buy that: "In a crowd, there's always someone pushing to be sensationalist. That's the poorest excuse in the world, to say others will run it or already have."

He gives an example from his days as an Associated Press reporter in Japan. "When John Lennon died, Yoko Ono's family lived down the road from me. The New York office requested I interview them. I refused. It would have been insensitive. I told the editors that the family couldn't have anything to say other than of sensationalistic value." Anderson preferred to respect the family's privacy. His editors backed off. Of course, not all reporters would have been able, or willing, to face down editors eager for a fresh angle on a major story.

Anderson's experiences shape his feelings on religion's role in public life, but he proffers a proviso regarding his captors: "The fact that my captors were Islamic fundamentalists is certainly less significant than the fact that they were extremists or terrorists. What they did in the name of Islam has been done in the name of Jesus. And Mohammed no more endorsed violence in the name of religion than did Jesus."

Anderson says that although he holds certain social values because of his religious beliefs, "I'm most vehemently against mixing religion and politics."

Is there common ground to be found? "Not only is there, but it's done very often," he points out. First, some preconceptions have to be overcome on both sides. The West, Anderson says, "looks at Muslims with a simplistic view and paints them with the brush of violence." The same occurs in the Muslim world, from the demonizing of America as the Great Satan by ayatollahs to the rejection of all things Western by certain fundamentalist sects.

"Much of the Muslim world has a distorted view of our society," says Anderson. He contends that polemics obscure the real issues, such as economic disparity and injustice. "The big differences are not between Islam and Christianity; the big differences are between rich and poor. And most of the world's Muslims are poor."

At home in the United States, Anderson worries about similar abuses in the name of religion.

"I am dismayed at the tendency to put political questions in religious terms and by the tendency of the religious right to arrogate political power to themselves. I'm amazed at seeing fundamentalist Christians attempting to coerce others who do not believe as they do or live as they do, whether they're on the school board trying to dictate what a course should contain or in the legislature trying to dictate what laws should be passed."

These biblically minded people, says Anderson, "should spend more time reading the New Testament than the Old Testament."

But don't strong religious beliefs necessarily translate into social and political causes and action? Many reforms now given the imprimatur of historical hindsight were born of religious conviction and, in their time, lambasted precisely as such. The abolitionists before the Civil War and many Civil Rights leaders were overtly religious, even ordained ministers. But in the eternal present, society is generally discomfited by those who take their beliefs *too* seriously, such as Native Americans who lie down in front of bulldozers to protect their sovereign homelands or antiabortionists who picket a clinic unceasingly. For Anderson, the public sphere is one of compromise, the forum where strong beliefs—personal, moral, spiritual—should be presented in more secular form for debate, compromise, synthesis.

"The primary thrust of religious beliefs should be private. I have enough trouble keeping my own life along Christian beliefs. The political system is there for a reason: to work out our differences. When positions are put in strictly religious terms, we can't compromise."

To help maintain his spiritual life, Anderson follows some basic practices. He attends Mass every Sunday and prays daily, "at odd times." He is frequently in other churches to give talks on his experience and various spiritual or social issues. He tries to base his decisions on his religious beliefs, primarily forgiveness, which he learned during and after his long captivity, when hate and resentment easily could have corroded his soul. He details this remarkable awakening, and others, in his memoir.

Today, he also speaks of the immense practicality of forgiving others. "If I don't forgive, it doesn't hurt those people; it hurts me. I have a wonderful life; I'm not going to poison it with anger. Forgiveness is a process—something you work on, think about, try to understand. Forgiveness is not about what they did; it's about me."

But acceptance and forgiveness do not amount to quietism and retreat. "What it doesn't mean is approval or acceptance of evil acts. I can forgive those men who kidnapped me and still accept that they should be punished and prevented from doing it again. I am not interested in tracking them down, but if one were picked up and brought to trial in the United States, I'd testify against him. It's justice.

"If I had one in my power, would I harm him? No. Revenge isn't justice." In this he echoes the New Testament stricture, "A man's anger does not serve God's justice."

Forgiveness, Anderson says, "is a liberating process." He finds encouragement and comfort in various readings. "I read the Bible, though not as much as I used to. I read other books, many of them on the church."

He recommends *An Ethic for Enemies: Forgiveness in Politics* by Donald W. Shriver, Jr., former president of Union Theological Seminary in New York, and also the memoir of his fellow captive, Father Lawrence Martin Jenco, *Bound to Forgive: The Pilgrimage to Reconciliation of a Beirut Hostage.*

"All the books by the hostages are different. They're about ourselves more than they are about the common events we experienced. Father Jenco was a kind, sweet, gentle and forgiving man. He was much more easily forgiving than I am. I have to work on it. He seemed to do it very easily."

Despite his dramatic experience and his inspiring tale,

told to audiences in churches and newspaper offices and banquets, Anderson declines to proselytize.

"I'm not an evangelist. I do take every opportunity to witness. People say they find it inspiring, but I am not trying to inspire people. I'm just trying to talk about what happened to me and what it meant." He and Madeleine, his wife and co-author, make the same point in their preface to *Den of Lions*, where they promise no lesson, no message other than that provided by the events they are about to recount.

Not that everyone needs to walk such a painful and extended *Via Dolorosa*.

"Though not many people get kidnapped, many, many people face those tests," Anderson argues. "Some of them have been writers and write very powerful things about it. It isn't necessary for all people to go through something like that to have a spiritual experience or to have a good relationship with God. People do that all the time. But it is true that those who have not developed that relationship properly can sometimes be shocked into it. It depends on one's ability to go inside oneself. Some can do it on their own and some have to be forced into it."

Writers or journalists can maintain their ethics and avoid professional exhaustion or burnout, Anderson says. Religious faith is not a necessity. "It's hard to keep your balance, but I know a lot of people who do. It has to do with your basic inner stability." Faith, however, can help and rarely hurts.

"I don't think having a solid religious faith is a handicap; it's an aid. Most of the senior journalists I know who are both sane and successful are people of fairly strong faith."

But it is in an arena other than daily journalism that he finds his current calling. "I don't miss it, not at all," he insists. "I don't want to get out there on the street again. That's a young man's work, a young woman's work."

All in all, Anderson speaks like a man comfortable with

himself, at peace with his life so far, his character, and any divide between his ideals and his reality. One suggestion of this self-acceptance lies in his comfort with silences.

Many reporters, in order to draw out interview subjects, will remain quiet after an answer and wait for the person to fill up the silence. Anderson, on the other hand, is sufficiently comfortable with the absence of words that he remains silent until asked another question.

His current life, which mixes public speaking, political reform, and writing columns, "is part of a spiritual journey that I am on," he says. "A priest I met in Wiesbaden, Germany, told me, 'God doesn't require you to reach the end of this journey immediately. He just wants you to be moving in that direction.'"

Acknowledgments

I thank my wife, Amy Biancolli Ringwald, for her love, editing and encouragement and my daughters, Madeleine Margaret and Jeanne Annemarie, for their smiles and shining eyes.

Thanks to those who first encouraged my writing, especially Tricia Sheehan Quinn, Raymond A. Schroth, S. J., Bryce Lambert, Michelle Scoville Burke, Lee Williams, Helen Wilson Chason and Bill Melvin. Thanks to my siblings and friends who helped us bury four family members and bear two new ones during the writing of this book. I appreciate Bill Droel of the National Center for the Laity, who steered me to ACTA Publications; Greg Pierce, the publisher who waited so long; and Francine O'Conner, who edited so well.

Finally, I am deeply grateful to the ten writers who opened their hearts, minds and souls to me and through this book, I trust, to many readers.

ALSO FROM ACTA PUBLICATIONS

The Legend of the Bells and Other Tales: Stories of the Human Spirit
by John Shea

Master storyteller and theologian John Shea offers 25 of his favorite stories, drawn from a variety of sources. Each is followed by Shea's thought-provoking reflection on the spiritual meaning of the story and its practical, personal relevance. (181 pages, $12.95)

Of Human Hands: A Reader in the Spirituality of Work
edited by Gregory F. Augustine Pierce

Essays by 22 different people on the spirituality that they find in their daily work, including reflections by a newspaper editor, a freelance writer, and an artist. (128 pages, $8.95)

The Spirituality of Work Series
by the National Center for the Laity

Eight booklets based on interviews with people in various occupations about the spirituality they find in their daily work. Includes *Teachers, Nurses, Business People, Homemakers, Lawyers, Unemployed Workers, Visual Artists* and *Military Personnel*. (48-64 pages each, $2.95).

The Waiting Place
by Barbara Ritter Garrison

An allegorical, metaphorical, mystical look at the mystery of daily life and the way God touches people through ordinary persons and events. A beautifully written book by a new writing talent. (112 pages, $5.95)

**Available from religious book sellers
or call 800-397-2282 in the U.S. or Canada.**

PN 4784.R3 R56 1997

DATE DUE